S·B·I
SMALL BUSINESS INSTITUTE

Advanced Simulation

COREL® WordPerfect® & Microsoft® Word

Ann P. Ambrose
Professor
Division of Business
Tidewater Community College
Portsmouth, VA

Dorothy L. R. Jones, Ph.D.
Associate Professor
Management Information Systems
Norfolk State University
Norfolk, VA

JOIN US ON THE INTERNET
WWW: http://www.thomson.com
EMAIL: findit@kiosk.thomson.com A service of I(T)P®

South-Western Educational Publishing
an International Thomson Publishing company I(T)P®

Cincinnati • Albany, NY • Belmont, CA • Bonn • Boston • Detroit • Johannesburg • London • Madrid
Melbourne • Mexico City • New York • Paris • Singapore • Tokyo • Toronto • Washington

Team Leader: Karen Schmohe
Project Manager: Inell Bolls
Editor: Kimberlee Kusnerak
Production Coordinator: Jane Congdon
Manufacturing Coordinator: Carol Chase
Marketing Manager: Tim Gleim
Marketing Coordinator: Lisa Barto
Art/Design Coordinator: Michelle Kunkler
Designer: Joe Pagliaro
Production: Douglas & Gayle Limited

I(T)P®
International Thomson Publishing
South-Western Educational Publishing is a division of International Thomson Publishing Inc. The ITP logo is a registered trademark used herein under license by South-Western Educational Publishing.

1 2 3 4 5 6 7 PR 02 01 00 99 98 97
Printed in the United States of America

Library of Congress Cataloging-in-Publication Data

Ambrose, Ann Peele,
SBI (Small Business Institute) : advanced simulation : COREL, Word Perfect/Microsoft Word / Ann P. Ambrose, Dorothy L.R. Jones.
p. cm.
ISBN 0-538-68387-2 (alk. paper)
1. Word processing--Simulation methods. 2. WordPerfect (Computer file) 3. Microsoft Word. I. Jones, Dorothy L. II. Title.
HF5548.115.A452 1999
652.5'5369--dc21 97-32091
CIP

Contents

Preface

About SBI

SBI (Small Business Institute) is a private nonprofit business advocacy organization in Raleigh, North Carolina, that provides support to small businesses that have the potential to expand. It provides management and technical assistance, private and public sector referrals, one-on-one marketing, and financial and international counseling to existing and start-up businesses. In short, **SBI** assists firms in their efforts to increase sales and profitability. More importantly, **SBI** uses one-year and long-range strategic planning to assist in carrying out its mission.

A myriad of management-assistance seminars, informational workshops, minority-issue seminars, international marketing and sales workshops, and business strategies seminars are provided by **SBI**. Once a year it sponsors an information and technology conference for its members. **SBI** is supported by its business, professional, and industrial member firms as well as government grants.

The Raleigh location employs eight professional employees, including the director, the administrative assistant, the program development manager, two technical assistants, an accountant, an office specialist, and a receptionist. It has a business membership of 548. A council that represents a broad cross-section of the membership governs the organization. It sets policies, establishes the budget, and oversees the work of the committees and task forces. The director is responsible for employing and managing the professional staff.

Mission Statement

The mission of **SBI** is to advance the commercial well-being of Raleigh-area small businesses by providing for economic expansion and serving the needs of member firms.

SBI ORGANIZATIONAL CHART

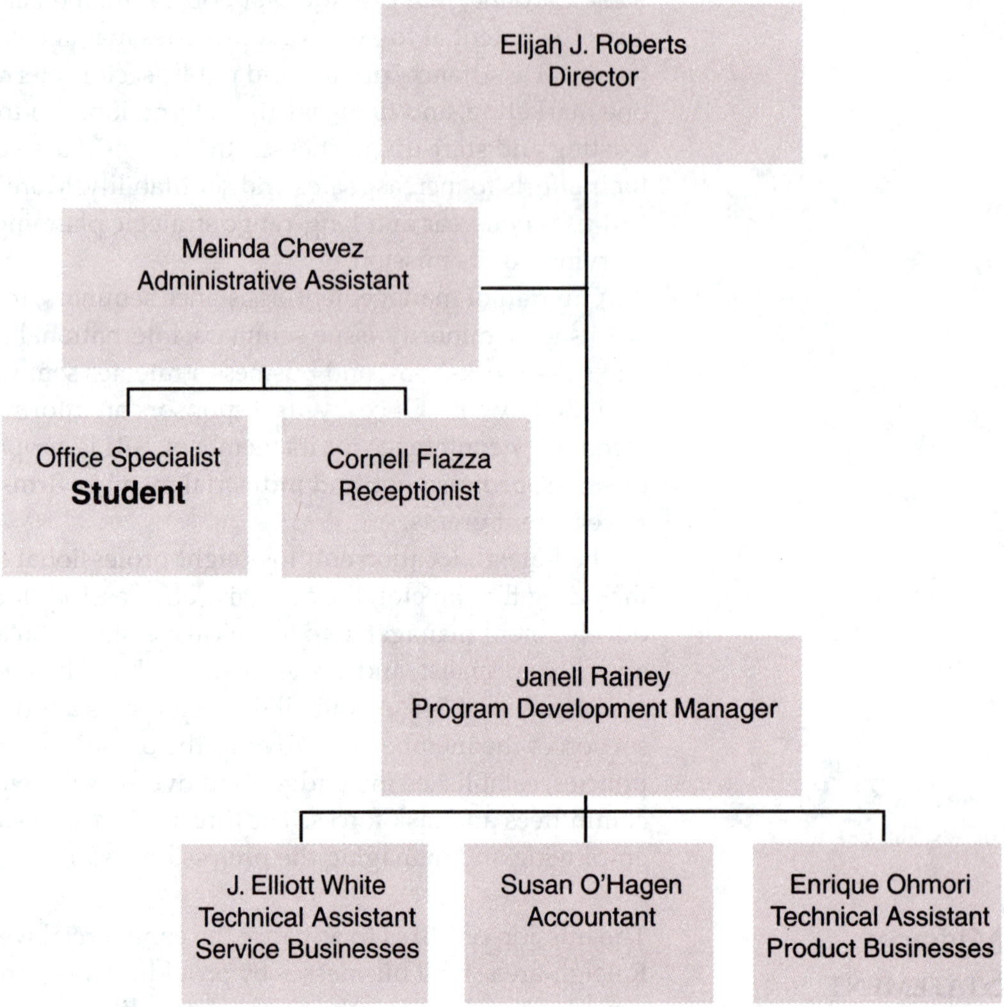

Office Specialist Job Description

Description

The Office Specialist provides program and operational support to the total organizational unit and performs work that emphasizes production, control, and general office and program support, individually or in combination. Some routine office, financial, and administrative responsibilities may be included. Work requires more specialized knowledge of office equipment capabilities and operations. Independence is allowed in determining work priorities and scheduling.

Complexity of Work

Work is of moderate difficulty and may be specialized or varied in nature. Some work requires discretion.

Performance Tasks

- Process reports and manuscripts of moderate complexity.
- Determine formats, establish and maintain computer files, and generate documents from stored data by inserting variables and manipulating text.
- Manipulate computer databases to store, retrieve, compile, or analyze information using COREL® WordPerfect® or Microsoft® Word for Windows®.
- Establish and maintain office filing system.
- Gather budget data, assist in routine personnel and financial transactions, keep non-complex personnel and fiscal records, and make routine purchases.
- Prepare and send correspondence and form letters on general matters.
- Compose documents on general matters.
- Edit and proofread materials for correct spelling and typographical and grammatical form.
- Prepare confidential material and ensure that all information is kept confidentially.

Knowledge, Skills, and Abilities

Working knowledge of office practices, procedures, and currently used office equipment; applicable laws, rules, and regulations pertaining to the supported activity; standard English grammar, punctuation, and usage; and basic computational skills.

Working skill in basic word processing and office suites software.

Demonstrated ability to interpret and follow oral and written rules and regulations; to function under difficult and high-pressure conditions; to maintain harmonious working relationships; to learn new practices, procedures, and equipment operations; to collect, assemble, and process information; and to organize work and make independent word processing decisions.

Overview of Simulation

SBI is an advanced word processing simulation. It is designed to reinforce your word processing skills as well as composition, critical thinking, and decision-making skills.

You will be working as an office specialist for the director of the **SBI** in Raleigh, North Carolina. As the office specialist, you will be responsible for preparing all word processing activities required by **SBI**. The simulation contains work for six weeks beginning January 6.

Your major responsibility in completing the simulation will be to assist with the preparations for the upcoming Conference and Expo that **SBI** is sponsoring. It will be held on May 8 and 9 at the Raleigh Suites and Convention Center. The theme of the conference is ***"Making the Small Business Connection."*** You will also be responsible for all word processing activities requested by the other employees.

You will mostly use the advanced functions of your word processing software. These include but are not limited to creating data files, merging files, creating tables, designing forms, inserting graphical elements, performing desktop publishing tasks, calculating data, creating templates and macros, using styles, and manipulating data.

You will incorporate and reinforce your academic skills, work in teams (cooperative learning), and develop an entrepreneurial spirit. More specifically, you will solve mathematical problems using formulas; compose business correspondence; analyze, evaluate, synthesize, and organize information from a variety of sources; work in teams to manipulate and organize data; and gain a basic understanding of several entrepreneurial concepts.

You will also have an opportunity to prepare an employment portfolio of your work. The purpose of the portfolio is to display the different types of documents that you are capable of preparing. You may want to store them in a three-ring binder with clear plastic page protectors. A copy of your resume should also be included in your portfolio. Many documents that you prepare in the completion of this simulation will have a portfolio icon, , indicating a document that should be displayed in your portfolio. You will be able to use this portfolio when you go on actual job interviews requiring word processing skill. Your instructor will give you more information on this portion of the simulation.

You should find completing the activities in this simulation unusually realistic and interesting because you will be given limited directions for completing the documents, as would be the case in a real office. Therefore, you will need to examine each document closely, read carefully whatever directions are given, and refer to the resources available in the simulation to process the documents. The activities in this simulation should provide you with valuable experience that you can apply in your business career.

Organization

This text-workbook includes a job description for the office specialist, pre-simulation activities, processing procedures for the simulation, template diskette instructions, job documents, and a reference manual. The simulation contains 32 jobs that require approximately 20-25 hours for completion or six weeks of work.

Key Features

- Reinforces advanced word processing skills such as merge, sort, columns, and formulas.
- Uses desktop publishing features.
- Uses software reference tools such as the spell checker, thesaurus, and grammar checker.
- Provides optional jobs, timed writings, and a test in the instructor's manual.
- Includes entrepreneurship concepts.
- Provides cooperative learning tasks.
- Provides for the integration of academic skills.
- Preparation of personal resume.
- Preparation of sample documents for employment portfolio.

Objectives

By completing this simulation, you will:

- reinforce your advanced word processing skills in processing documents such as letters, memos, reports, tables, programs, and newsletters.
- use advanced software features such as merge, sort, columns, graphics, formulas, macros, and tables of contents.
- retrieve and edit stored files.
- work from a variety of inputs.

- compose documents from several different resources.
- create and use software templates.
- use desktop publishing features.
- compose "good news" and "bad news" correspondence.
- work independently in making decisions.
- work as part of a team.
- use various software tools such as the spell checker, the grammar checker, and the thesaurus.

Pre-Simulation Activities

- Write your name in appropriate spaces in this text/workbook.
- Preview the Reference Manual to become familiar with the various procedures you will follow in completing jobs in this simulation as well as the document formats that are used at **SBI**.
- Format a blank diskette, if necessary, so that you will have it ready when you need to use it for storing your work.
- Have the following supplies available: (Your instructor will give specific directions regarding these.)
  - Envelopes (No. 10)
  - Labels (optional)
  - Resume bond paper (optional)
  - A blank diskette

Processing Procedures

Below are directions for completing the jobs in this simulation.

1. *Read each job very carefully. Consult the Reference Manual and other resources as needed to obtain the information you need to complete your assignments.*
2. *Use the following "icons," which appear on some jobs, to aid you in completing the jobs.*

   (Diskette) *The diskette icon indicates a file that you will need to retrieve to complete the job. (The directory [folder] will not be listed.)*

(Book)	*The book icon represents the Reference Manual and indicates that you are to refer to it for formatting information.*
(Telephone)	*The telephone icon represents a hint for preparing the document.*
(Envelope)	*The envelope icon indicates that you are to key an envelope.*
(Labels)	*The label icon indicates that you are to key labels.*

3. *Proofread, spell check, and correct jobs before printing and submitting.*
4. *Save each job using the filename that has been provided. You are to save each file in the directory (folder) of the person for whom you are keying the job. (Example: If you are keying a document for Melinda Chevez and will save it as "smith," the complete path, if you are saving it on Drive A, would be A:\chevez\smith.) Your instructor may give you additional directions. Please remember to save your work frequently.*
5. *Key the complete path name for the file in the lower left corner in a 10-point font on each document for identification purposes. You may use the file stamp command, if your software has that option, or insert the filename manually or in a footer.*

   Note: *In business, the file-stamp information is keyed only on the file copy of the document and not on the original.*
6. *Key your reference initials on all letters and memos.*
7. *Create a directory (folder) for the person for whom you are to key documents, if they do not already have one on the template diskette.*
8. *Use the template file called "ltrhead" for all letters.*
9. *Record the completion date for each job on the Job Log, which is found on page 119 in the Reference Manual in this workbook.*
10. *Record your grade in the appropriate space on the Job Log when you receive it from your instructor. Your instructor will give you directions for submitting your work.*
11. *Make the necessary corrections, after you have received your graded paper from your instructor, to the jobs that are to be included in your portfolio. Print a new copy, even if there were no errors, and place it in your portfolio.*
12. *Use two spaces after end-of-sentence punctuation in documents except in desktop publishing documents—the newsletter and conference program.*

TEMPLATE DISKETTE INSTRUCTIONS

Template Files and Directories/Folders

Eight template files have been provided for your use in completing this simulation. A directory for both Word and WordPerfect is included on the template. Directories (folders) have been created for persons who have documents stored on the diskette. Your instructor will provide you with directions for accessing these files.

The following directories (folders) and files are on the diskette.

CHEVEZ

conregis.xxx*	Registration form for the conference.
ly_vendb.dat	Database of last year's vendors.
mentor.xxx	Draft of a study on Small Business Owner Mentorship Initiative.
profile.xxx	A file of information about the luncheon and banquet speakers.
semtopic.xxx	A file of the descriptions of all workshops.

OHAGEN

crsrev3.xxx	A document showing the revenue from third quarter courses.

TEMPLATE

ltrhead.xxx	A template of the letterhead that is to be used for all letters.
logo.xxx	SBI logo.

*.*xxx* represents the software file extension, for example, *.doc* or *.wpd*.

Jobs

S·B·I

SMALL BUSINESS INSTITUTE

Melinda Chevez, Administrative Assistant

January 6, ----

Please retrieve this file and make the indicated changes. Modify to fit on one page. You may need to change the spacing between each topic. Sort based on paragraphs to put workshop topics in alphabetical order. (Do not include the Pre-Conference workshops; these are to remain at the end of the list.)

2714 Spring Forest Road
Raleigh, NC 27610-1997
(919) 555-0126

(Job 1 continued on p. 14.)

Hint: "Make It Fit" or "Shrink to Fit" Command

Filename: semtopic

SEMINAR TOPICS

How to Get Free Promotion and Publicity

Free publicity from the news media is an effective to influence the opinions of your customers. This seminar explains how, when, and where to send the news release, how to approach and understand media people, and most importantly, how to determine what is newsworthy. It will also suggest ways to create your own newsworthy events.

Protecting Your Personnel Investment

An examination of productive personnel management through the reduction of absenteeism and tardiness and the building of employee morale. The concept and steps of Employee Assistance Programming designed to salvage valuable employees and lower operating costs will be examined.

Customer Satisfaction Program/Handling Customer Complaints

A satisfied customer is a profitable customer. Learn to analyze your firm, identify customer needs and maximize customer satisfaction. A satisfied customer is your most effective salesperson. The most effective ways to eliminate customer complaints and turn complaining customers into satisfied ones will be discussed.

Introduction to Export Marketing

The purpose of this workshop is to acquaint interested persons with export sales, planning, financing, and documentation. In addition, sources of state and federal assistance in exporting will also be discussed.

Keeping a Successful Attitude

Definite skills and techniques to overcome negativism that bombards you daily. Not just a pump-up session. A systematic approach towards maintaining a positive attitude in your personal and professional life.

Bidding and Quoting on Government Small Purchases

Private sector insights on bidding and quoting on small purchases will be explored along with a representative from the Navy explaining small purchase procedures.

Techniques for Collecting Accounts Receivable

--Proven Telephone Collection Techniques
--Specific Skills for Successful Negotiating
--Maximizing the Impact of Collecting Letters
--Effective Collection Strategies
--Special Arrangements to Guarantee Payment
--Using Collection Laws to Your Advantage

Planning and Budgeting--How to Survive in Business

Effective planning and budgeting are very vital aspects of a successful business. Learn strategies that you empower you to ensure the success of you business.

Developing a Marketing Plan for the Small Business

There's more to marketing your business than advertising in the local paper, or placing an ad in the telephone book. Learn proven techniques for marketing your business successfully.

Pre-Conference Workshops

Marketing Your Business on the Internet

Creating a Home Page for Your Business

A:\chevez\semtopic

S·B·I
SMALL BUSINESS INSTITUTE

Melinda Chevez, Administrative Assistant

January 7, ----

Please prepare the attached flyer for announcing one of the workshop sessions at the "Making the Small Business Connection" Conference and Expo. Please use your judgment as far as font styles, font sizes, lines, etc. Arrange attractively. If you wish, you may use a different border as well as additional graphics. Be sure to include all information shown.

2714 Spring Forest Road
Raleigh, NC 27610-1997
(919) 555-0126

Reference Manual: Flyer Format

A Workshop

on

Developing a Marketing Plan for the Small Business

is scheduled
for

Thursday, May 8, ----
3:30 p.m. – 4:45 p.m.
at
Raleigh Suites and Convention Center

Presented by The Small Business Institute

S·B·I
SMALL BUSINESS INSTITUTE

Melinda Chevez, Administrative Assistant

January 7, ----

Use the attached list to create a merge data file for the speakers who will be participating in the "Making the Small Business Connection" Conference and Expo.

Use the following fields:

title	first name	last name	company
address	city	state	postal code

Save the file as "wkspldrs."

2714 Spring Forest Road
Raleigh, NC 27610-1997
(919) 555-0126

~~SPEAKERS~~ Workshop Leaders

1. Linda Adams, Esq.
Adams Financial Services
129 Fairlawn Drive
Raleigh, NC 27609-1786

2. Mr. Harry Walker
Walker Enterprises
4516 Second Avenue
Durham, NC 27701-3781

3. Dr. Vivian Matthews
4329 Douglas Court
Raleigh, NC 27608-1894

4. Ms. Donna Sawyer
Telenet Services, Inc.
1405 New Charles Street
Raleigh, NC 27604-1999

5. Miss Marsh~~a~~e Armstrong
Tri-Cities Chamber of Commerce
857 Spence Circle
Durham, NC 27705-3384

6. Ms. Phoebe Hernandez
Hernandez Marketing Services
703 Thimble Street
Durham, NC 27715-3201

To create fields.
Tools
merge
Data file

(Job 3 continued on p. 20.)

DATA file on one page

7. Mr. Wilson Moretz
Moretz Graphics
1405 Westover Hills Boulevard
Durham, NC 27706-3784

8. Mrs. Tien S. Sheng
City of Raleigh
Municipal Center Building #5
Raleigh, NC 27610-1949

THINGS TO DO TODAY

January 9, ----

Priority	Task to Be Completed	Completed
a	Create a signature block macro for the	
	director & one for Melinda. Use their	
	last names as the filenames for their	
	macro. Use these macros when keying	
	their letters.	
a	Edit a memo template in your software	
	to include SBI's logo to use when	
	keying memos. Save new ~~memo~~ template	
	as "memotemp" in the template directory.	

facsimile
TRANSMITTAL

to: Office Specialist

fax #: (919) 555-0112

re: Conference Registration Form

date: January 13, ----

pages: 3, including this cover sheet

I am sending you a rough draft of the registration form. I took it with me to my meeting and had time to fill in the rest of the program. Please retrieve the file and complete the brochure. If you have questions, I will be in early tomorrow.

Melinda

path + file name.

Filename: conregis

PARTICIPANTS

List the names of the workshop leaders here; include their organization. Retrieve appropriate file to get this information.

Pg 19

To register for this exciting conference and Expo, complete and detach the registration form below and mail with your payment to:

SBI
2714 Spring Forest Road
Raleigh, NC 27610-1997

"MAKING THE SMALL BUSINESS CONNECTION"
CONFERENCE & EXPO

REGISTRATION FORM

Company's Name ______________________________ Phone ______________

Address ____ ZIP ____________

Individual's Name and Title ____

Registrations _____ @ $99 = $_______

_____ @ $79 = $_______ (for 2 or more persons from same company)

Total Enclosed $_______

_____ Check made payable to SBI _____Purchase Order #_________

Format attractively!

MAKING
THE
SMALL BUSINESS CONNECTION
Conference and Expo

insert an appropriate graphic or other design element!

presented
by

SBI
Small Business Institute

May 8 & 9, ---- ← appropriate year!

(Job 5 continued on p. 24.)

SBI
Small Business Institute

proudly presents

"MAKING THE SMALL BUSINESS CONNECTION"
Conference and Expo

Plan to join us and learn how you can make your small business survive and thrive. Below is a list of the workshops that will be presented.

Bidding and Quoting on Government Small Purchases
Customer Satisfaction Program/Handling Customer Complaints
Developing a Marketing Plan for the Small Business
How to Get Free Promotion and Publicity
Introduction to Export Marketing
Keeping a Successful Attitude
Planning and Budgeting--How to Survive in Business
Protecting Your Personnel Investment
Techniques for Collecting Accounts Receivable

BONUS PRE-CONFERENCE WORKSHOPS

Marketing Your Business on the Internet
Creating a Home Page for Your Business

HOTEL ACCOMMODATIONS

A special rate of $75 per night has been secured for participants attending the conference here at the Raleigh Suites and Convention Center. If you would like to reserve a room, call the hotel directly at 1-800-555-0199.

PROGRAM

Thursday, May 8

8:00 a.m. - 12:00 noon	Registration
9:00 a.m. - 11:30 a.m.	Pre-Conference Workshops Creating a Home Page for Your Business Marketing Your Business on the Internet
12 noon - 1:00 p.m.	Opening Session and Luncheon Ms. Roberta Sanchez, Speaker President, Sanchez Financial Services
2:00 p.m. - 3:15 p.m.	Concurrent Sessions
3:30 p.m. - 4:45 p.m.	Concurrent Sessions
5:30 p.m. - 6:30 p.m.	Business Networking and Card Exchange
6:30 p.m. - 8:30 p.m.	Banquet Mr. Ben Suggs, Speaker Chairman & CEO, Suggs Technology Corp. spell out!

Friday, May 9

7:30 a.m. - 8:30 a.m.	Continental Breakfast
8:45 a.m. - 10:00 a.m.	Concurrent Sessions
10:15 a.m. - 11:30 a.m.	Concurrent Sessions
11:30 a.m. - 12:00 noon	Refreshments & Checkout
12:15 - 1:30 p.m.	Closing Session and Luncheon Mr. Anthony Hertz, II, Speaker Creative Director Internet Connections

S·B·I

SMALL BUSINESS INSTITUTE

Melinda Chevez, Administrative Assistant

January 14, ----

Please retrieve last year's vendor data file (ly_vendb) and update it based on the attached printout. Save the updated file as "vendrdbf." Print one copy of the file.

Perform a query based upon the field "company;" sort in ascending order. Save the query as "vendlst." Print one copy of the query.

2714 Spring Forest Road
Raleigh, NC 27610-1997
(919) 555-0126

(Job 6 continued on p. 26.)

Filename: ly_vendb

Title	FirstName	LastName	Company	Address1	City	State	PostalCode
Miss	Marshe	Armstrong	Armstrong Associates	8011 Villa Park Drive	Raleigh	NC	27603-1656
Ms	Lois	Ashburne	Kanawha Medical Supply, Inc	1405 Westover Hills Boulevard	Raleigh	NC	27609-1265
Mr	Scott	Ayers	Leading Edge Realty	4772 Euclid Road	Raleigh	NC	27610-1999
Ms	Susan	Banks	Green Graphics	3301 Thomas Street	Raleigh	NC	27654-1451
Mr	Thomas	Berry	Laverne's Florist	3500 Chestnut Avenue	Raleigh	NC	27605-1876
Ms	Laverne	Britt	Internet Resource Group	101 Tomaras Avenue	Raleigh	NC	27608-1455
Mrs	Addie	Burkins	Computek	3294 Burns Court	Raleigh	NC	27609-1998
Mr	Raeshay	Cooper	Watson Incorporated	78 Crashaw Street	Raleigh	NC	27601-1462
Mr	Tim	Croston	New Beginnings Barber and Style Shop	9402 Ransdell Road	Raleigh	NC	27601-1458
Mr	James	Davenport	Diezewl Associates	7865 Fourth Street	Raleigh	NC	27602-1563
Ms	Cindy	Davis	GIS Solutions	108th Avenue, NE	Raleigh	NC	27615-1320
Mr	William	Delane	Business Services Unlimited	PO Box 1097	Raleigh	NC	27607-1254
Mr	Martine	England	A to Z Typing Services	4879 Yorkshire Lane	Raleigh	NC	27603-1656
Mr	Shelton	Hill	African Trends	1120 S City Hall Avenue	Raleigh	NC	27619-1363
Mrs	Barbara	Johnson	Invisions Optometrist	1234 St Paul Boulevard	Raleigh	NC	27608-1456
Mr	Charles	Jones	Goodman Books, Inc	12 Second Street	Durham	NC	27709-3362
Mrs	Jane	Keller	Tools, Techniques, Inc	7893 Windson Boulevard	Raleigh	NC	27603-1921
Dr	Bob	Kotalik	Best Enterprises	1346 South Hampton Avenue	Raleigh	NC	27603-1621
Dr	Daisy	Leon	Allen Accounting Services	224 W Princess Anne Avenue	Raleigh	NC	27607-1321
Mr	Christian	Lopez	Cooper Consultants	908 Creenshaw Avenue	Durham	NC	27713-3337
Mr	Lei	Lu	Max Environmental Company	703 Thimble Road	Raleigh	NC	27610-1567
Miss	Rosa	Mendez	Water Solutions	857 Spence Circle	Durham	NC	27708-3356
Mr	Hector	Ortiz	Whitman and Associates	9874 Arlington Avenue	Durham	NC	27701-3334
Ms	Karen	Pearson	Ryals Company	One Chambers Court	Raleigh	NC	27610-1110
Miss	Kristen	Thomas	Protective Innovations	3 Otsego Drive	Durham	NC	27704-3342
Mr	Louis	White	TBC and Company	5045 Admiral Wright Road	Raleigh	NC	27603-1811

S·B·I
SMALL BUSINESS INSTITUTE

To: Office Specialist Date: Jan. 15

( ) Please investigate and return to me.
( ) Please correct.
( ) Please take charge of this.
(✓) Please prepare for my signature.
( ) Please select ____ records and print.
( ) Please prepare a response.

COMMENTS

Key the attached letter as a form file and merge with the "vendrdbf" file. Print the first letter only. Also prepare a set of mailing labels. Save labels as "vendlbl."
Save the form file as "vendltr."
Don't save the merged letters.

Elijah Roberts
Signature

(Job 7 continued on p. 28.)

Labels

Thank you for agreeing to participate in Making the Small Business Connection Conference and Expo on May 8 and 9. We are anticipating an exciting event for the Small Business Institute and the community at large.

The following information should be most helpful:

- You have been assigned a booth in Ballroom D at the Raleigh Suites and Convention Center. You can begin setting up any time after 7 a.m. on Thursday, May 8.

- You have reserved seating at the luncheon on Friday. To secure your tickets, please report to Guest Relations.

- A map of the Convention Center is enclosed for your convenience.

We are looking forward to a great conference, and your presence and support will add so much to making this a successful endeavor. If you need additional information, please call (919) 555-0126, or send an e-mail message to sbi@aadj.rxc.org.

Type letter.

S·B·I
SMALL BUSINESS INSTITUTE

Melinda Chevez, Administrative Assistant

January 16, ----

Please key the attached summer schedule. It will be included in RCC's summer schedule book; hence, it should look as attractive as possible. You may key the schedule in portrait or landscape orientation; however, it must fit on one page. You may also include the SBI logo. Compose a letter for my signature to:

Mrs. Betty Swain, Chairperson
Business Division
Raleigh Community College
5000 College Drive
Raleigh, NC 27606-0212

Inform her that this is the schedule we would like included in their summer schedule book.
Save the schedule as "sumsch98," and the letter as "bswain."

2714 Spring Forest Road
Raleigh, NC 27610-1997
(919) 555-0126

(Job 8 continued on p. 30.)

Hint: Use the table feature for the schedule.

SBI

add address and tele. #

(key year) ---- Summer Class Schedule

Date	Days	Course Title	Time	Room	Cost
June 2 & 4	MW	Windows 95	6:00 p.m.– ~~6:00 a.m.~~ 9:30 p.m.	C21	$ 50
June 3 & 5	TR	Windows 3.1	6:00 a.m.– 9:30 p.m.	C21	$ 50
June 9, 11, 16, 18	MW	WordPerfect 6.1	" "	C23	$100
June 10, 12, 17, 19	TR	WordPerfect 7.0	" "	C23	$100
June 16, 18, 23, 25	MW	MS Word 7.0	" "	C20	$100
June 18, 20, 25, 27	WF	MS Excel 7.0	4:30 p.m.– 6:30 p.m.	C22	$ 50
June 21 & 28	S	MS Excel 7.0	9:00 a.m.– 1:00 p.m.	C20	$ 50
July 7, 9, 14, 16	MW	MS Access 7.0	6:00 p.m.– 9:30 p.m.	C21	$100
July 19 & 26	S	MS Access 7.0	9:00 a.m.– 1:00 p.m.	C21	$ 50
July 8, 10, 15, 17	TR	MS PowerPoint 7.0	6:30 p.m.– 9:30 p.m.	C22	$ 75
July 21, 23, 28, 30	MW	Lotus for Windows R5	" "	C21	$ 75
August 5 & 6	MW	Planning to Go into Business	4:30 p.m.– 6:30 p.m.	B6	$ 50
August 12 & 14	MW	Knowing Your Market	" "	B6	$ 50
August 20 & 22	TR	Money: Getting It and Keeping Track of It.	" "	B6	$ 50
August 27 & 29	TR	Your Business and the Law	" "	B6	$ 50

To Register: Call SBI at 555-0126. You will be given directions for registering for any of the above courses. Class size is limited, so register early.

M=Monday T=Tuesday W=Wednesday R=Thursday F=Friday

S·B·I
SMALL BUSINESS INSTITUTE

Melinda Chevez, Administrative Assistant

January 16, ----

Use the table feature to create the attached list of publications. Change fonts and margins to make sure that all information fits on one page. Make sure that the list will be ready for distribution at the "Making the Small Business Connection" Conference and Expo on May 8 and 9.

Save the file as "publist."

2714 Spring Forest Road
Raleigh, NC 27610-1997
(919) 555-0126

(Job 9 continued on p. 32.)

Hint: Do not shade more than 30 percent.

SBI PUBLICATIONS		Price
☐ ***Starting and Managing a Small Business***. The dream of creating and leading a successful enterprise depends upon the practical aspects of such a venture, including the risks, discussed in this Starting and Managing series pamphlet.		
60 pages	S/N 044-098-003217-8	$5.25
☐ ***Buying and Selling a Small Business***. Going into business for oneself can be a great adventure or a great disaster. This booklet serves as a guide to areas needing investigation by the buyer and the seller and suggests some approaches that may be helpful in obtaining necessary information.		
145 pages	S/N 044-098-003217-9	$8.99
☐ ***Exporting Marketing for Smaller Firms***. This booklet outlines what a small firm needs to know to determine whether it should consider exporting its goods or services.		
40 pages	S/N 044-987-345912-4	$3.75
☐ ***Selling to the United States Government***. This booklet is the small business firm's key to government contracting. It outlines basic information needed in selling to the United States government and describes ways SBI helps small businesses over contracting roadblocks.		
55 pages	S/N 044-786-234569-6	$4.99
☐ ***A Handbook of Small Business Finance***. This booklet provides a starting point for small business owners or managers who want to sharpen their financial management skills.		
158 pages	S/N 044-123-456780-3	$9.85
☐ ***Managing the Small Business Firm for Growth and Profit***. This publication will help business owners gain a better understanding of what is to be done to find business opportunities that are compatible with their objectives and experience and that offer good profit potential as well.		
123 pages	S/N 044-000-567834-2	$6.50

DO NOT DETACH—RETURN ENTIRE FORM

Mail to:
Small Business Institute
2714 Spring Forest Road
Raleigh, NC 27610-1997

Enclosed is $________(check or money order payable to SBI. Please do not send cash or stamps.)

Name ________________________________

Street Address ________________________________

City, State, and ZIP ________________________________

DO NOT DETACH—RETURN ENTIRE FORM

S·B·I
SMALL BUSINESS INSTITUTE

Susan O'Hagen, Accountant

January 19, ----

Please retrieve this file and complete the computations. (Revenue = Enrollment X Cost per Student) Use 10 percent shading in the title row and a double outside border.

2714 Spring Forest Road
Raleigh, NC 27610-1997
(919) 555-0126

(Job 10 continued on p. 34.)

Filename: crsrev3

SMALL BUSINESS INSTITUTE

Summary of Computer Courses ~~Offered~~ *Revenue*

Third Quarter, ----

	Course Title	Sessions	Enrollment	Cost Per Student	Revenue
1	WordPerfect 6.1 for Windows	3	57	$95	$
2	WordPerfect 6.0 for DOS	2	23	$50	
3	Microsoft Windows 3.1	7	111	$50	
4	Microsoft Windows 95	6	97	$50	
5	Microsoft Word 6.0	3	47	$95	
6	Microsoft Word 7.0	4	47	$95	
7	Microsoft Excel 7.0	6	101	$50	
8	Microsoft Access 7.0	4	80	$50	
9	Microsoft PowerPoint 7.0	3	58	$90	
10	Quicken *Deluxe*	2	33	$50	
11	Quattro Pro *7.0*	2	19	$90	
12	Desktop Publishing	4	71	$90	
13	dBase III+	2	27	$50	
14	Microsoft Project Manager	3	43	$50	↓
	TOTALS				

S·B·I
SMALL BUSINESS INSTITUTE

Melinda Chevez, Administrative Assistant

January 20, ----

Please compose a letter to the cleaning contractor expressing our displeasure with their work. You may cite the following:

1. All trash cans are not being emptied.
2. Objects are not being moved so that dusting is complete.
3. Candy is missing from offices.
4. Radios in offices are being played; stations are being changed.

Request that performance be improved; if not, our contract will be terminated. Prepare for my signature.

Mr. Joseph Knight
White Knight Cleaning Services
613 Oakside Crossing
Raleigh, NC 27613-1967

Save the file as "cleaning."

2714 Spring Forest Road
Raleigh, NC 27610-1997
(919) 555-0126

job 12

S·B·I
SMALL BUSINESS INSTITUTE

Elijah Roberts, Director

January 21, ----

Please use the attached figures to prepare my expense report for attending the regional meeting in Greenville, NC.

Print two copies.

Save the file as "reptexp"

2714 Spring Forest Road
Raleigh, NC 27610-1997
(919) 555-0126

Hint: Use the expense report template if it is available in your software. If it is not, create the information using the table feature.

EXPENSE REPORT

Fax:

EMPLOYEE NAME	Elijah Roberts
EMPLOYEE TITLE	Director
DEPARTMENT	
BUILDING	
TELEPHONE	555-0126
SUPERVISOR	
PURPOSE OF TRIP	Attend Regional Meeting

Date	Description	Travel	Lodging	Breakfast	Lunch	Dinner	Transport	Entertain	Other	TOTALS
1-10	Registration (other)	291.00	97.00	--	18.87	28.33	--	--	75.00	
1-11			97.00	9.76	16.19	30.21				
1-12			97.00	9.76	13.76	27.14				
1-13				8.53	--	--				
	TOTALS									**0.00**
									Advances and charges to company	
										$0.00
										TOTAL

Employee Signature *Date*

Approved By *Date*

S·B·I
SMALL BUSINESS INSTITUTE

Melinda Chevez, Administrative Assistant

January 22, ----

We need to put the teaching contracts on the computer. Key the attached copy of our teaching contract as a template file. You will use it later to prepare individual contracts.

Save the file as "teachcon."

2" left aligned

2714 Spring Forest Road
Raleigh, NC 27610-1997
(919) 555-0126

S·B·I
SMALL BUSINESS INSTITUTE

TEACHING CONTRACT

Name: Date:

Social Security Number: Term:

No. of Courses: Salary:

The Institute reserves the right to cancel any class prior to the time that the class next meets following the drop/add session in which the class begins. There are no provisions for payment for partial services in the event the class is canceled.

Acceptance of this contract includes acceptance of the general conditions of employment set forth in the policy manual of the Small Business Institute and the faculty handbook. Incompetence, inadequate or unsatisfactory performance of duties, insubordination, or misconduct is grounds for immediate removal.

Special Conditions: ____

____

If the terms of this appointment are acceptable to you, please sign, date, and return the original and one copy of this proposal to the administrative office. You will NOT be placed on the payroll until the signed contract has been returned.

Title of Course	Course Code	Lecture Hours	Lab Hours	Total Credit Hours

Rate Per Credit Hour $: _____ X Credit Hours: _____ = $ ______ Total Gross Salary

______________________ 2" L. 4.5" ______________________ 2" Right.

Director Appointee

Date:______________________ Date:______________________

Paid on Voucher Number: __________ Check Date:____________________

Full justified

THINGS TO DO TODAY

January 26, ----

Priority	Task to Be Completed	Completed
B	Write memo to staff to tell them to	
	schedule their evaluations w/ Melinda.	
	The evaluations will take place the	
	week of Feb. 9. They are to	
	schedule w/ me by Feb. 2. (Per Roberts).	
	Remind them to bring their self	
	evaluations with them to their	
	evaluation session.	
	Save file as "evalmemo."	

S·B·I
SMALL BUSINESS INSTITUTE

Melinda Chevez, Administrative Assistant

January 26, ----

Please retrieve the sumsch98 file and add a column between the course title column and the time column to add a column for the course number. The course numbers are listed on the attached sheet.

Save this file as "ssch98-1."

Sumsch2000-1

2714 Spring Forest Road
Raleigh, NC 27610-1997
(919) 555-0126

(Job 15 continued on p. 42.)

Filename: sumsch98

Course Numbers

Windows 95	CQ011-01
Windows 3.1	CQ012-01
WordPerfect 6.1	~~CQ10~~ CQ013-01
WordPerfect 7.0	CQ014-01
MS Word 7.0	CQ015-01
MS Excel 7.0	CQ016-01
MS Excel 7.0	CQ016-02
MS Access 7.0	CQ017-01
MS Access 7.0	CQ017-02
MS PowerPoint 7.0	CQ018-01
Lotus	CQ019-01
Planning to Go Into Business	BW27
Knowing Your Market	BW29
Money: Getting It and Keeping Track of It	BW28
Your Business and the Law	BW17

S·B·I
SMALL BUSINESS INSTITUTE

Melinda Chevez, Administrative Assistant

January 27, ----

Key the attached outline. Prepare a header for the second page. It is to include the title of the outline as well as the page number.

Save the file as "busplan."

2714 Spring Forest Road
Raleigh, NC 27610-1997
(919) 555-0126

(Job 16 continued on p. 44.)

Reference Manual: Outline Format

SAMPLE BUSINESS PLAN OUTLINE

I. Cover Letter ← CAPS

DS

A. Dollar amount requested
B. Terms and timing
C. Type and price of securities

II. Summary

A. Business description
   1. Name
   2. Location and plant description
   3. Product
   4. Market and competition
   5. Management expertise

B. Business Goals
C. Summary of financial needs and application of funds
D. Earnings projections and potential return to investors

III. Market Analysis

A. Description of total market
B. Industry trends
C. Target market
D. Competition

IV. Products or Services

A. Description of product line
B. Proprietary position: patents, copyrights, and legal and technical considerations
C. Comparison to competitors' products

V. Manufacturing Process (if applicable)

A. Materials
B. Source of supply
C. Production methods

VI. Marketing Strategy

A. Overall strategy
B. Pricing policy
C. Method of selling, distributing, and servicing products.

VII. Management Plan

A. Form of business organization
B. Board of directors composition
C. Officers: organization chart and responsibilities
D. Resumes of key personnel
E. Staffing plan/number of employees
F. Facilities plan/planned capital improvements
G. Operating plan/schedule of upcoming work for next one to two years.

VIII. Financial Data

A. Financial statements (five years to present)
B. Five-year financial projections (first year by quarters; remaining years annually)
   1. Profit and loss statements
   2. Balance sheets
   3. Cash flow charts
   4. Capital expenditure estimates
C. Explanation of projections
D. Key business ratios
E. Explanation of use and effect of new funds
F. Potential return to investors; comparison to average return in the industry as a whole.

S·B·I
SMALL BUSINESS INSTITUTE

J. Elliott White, Technical Assistant for Service Businesses

January 28, ----

Please key this schedule using an appropriate format. Try to fit on one page. Use various font sizes and font styles. Format attractively.

Save the file as: "succprog."

2714 Spring Forest Road
Raleigh, NC 27610-1997
(919) 555-0126

written on line paper

SMALL BUSINESS START-UP stet

Danielle Reid, Ph.D.

Associate Professor and Director, Small Business Resource Center

Saint Augustine University

SCHEDULE

Saturday, May 8

8:30 a.m.–9:45 a.m. Introduction
Course Objectives/Expectations

9:45 a.m.–10:00 a.m. Break

10:00 a.m.–12:00 noon Entrepreneurship and Small Business
~~1:00~~ Enterprise: Expectations & Requirements
~~1:00–2:30 p.m.~~

12:00 p.m.–1:00 p.m. Lunch

1:00 p.m.–2:30 p.m. Beginning the Small Business Enterprise

2:30 p.m.–2:45 p.m. Break

2:45 p.m.–4:45 p.m. Legal Structure: Possibilities,
Advantages & Disadvantages of Each

Sunday, May 9

8:30 a.m.–12:00 noon Small Business Financing: Needs,
Sources and Problems

12:00 p.m.–1:00 p.m. Lunch

1:00 p.m.–4:30 p.m. Small Business Management: Key
Concepts
(2:30 p.m. – 2:45 p.m. – Break)

4:30 p.m. – 5:30 p.m. Summary and Evaluation

job 18

S·B·I
SMALL BUSINESS INSTITUTE

Janell Rainey, Program Development Manager

January 29, ----

Please key the attached course outline. Use your own judgment along with the Reference Manual info for formatting.

You may add a heading with the SBI logo if you wish. Key the description and outline on separate sheets. (Remember to key the title of the course on both the outline and the description.)

Thanks.

Save the file as "jobeval."

2714 Spring Forest Road
Raleigh, NC 27610-1997
(919) 555-0126

Add = header.

LOGO

JOB EVALUATION AND WAGE ADMINISTRATION

Objectives

- To present the principles of several of the more important job evaluation techniques. Emphasis is placed upon the point system.

- To show how job evaluation systems can be valuable aids in making wage decisions.

- To give participants sufficient background to choose a job evaluation plan to suit their needs and experience in the responsibilities of an evaluation committee.

Workshop Description

Job evaluation is a highly recognized and valuable system for analyzing the factors that constitute a job for the purpose of determining an equitable rate of pay. In the absence of such a system, pay rates become out of line within the community and the organization. This results in employee dissatisfaction, lower-quality performance, and the inability to attract and hold competent personnel. Various plans will be examined with emphasis upon the popular "point-type" plans. Factor selection, weights, and steps will be emphasized. An exercise in job rating and classification is an important part of this workshop. This is not a workshop on how to write a job description, although this topic will be dealt with to the extent necessary to understand good job evaluation procedures.

This workshop is designed for those who assist with the writing of job descriptions, serve on rating committees, or have the responsibility of explaining compensation practices to subordinates, but it is not intended for the seasoned compensation administrator.

(Job 18 continued on p. 50.)

LOGO

JOB EVALUATION AND WAGE ADMINISTRATION

I. DEFINITION OF JOB EVALUATION

II. BENEFITS OF JOB EVALUATION AND WAGE ADMINISTRATION

A. Job Evaluation
B. Wage Administration Clarified

III. FOUR STEPS IN JOB EVALUATION

A. Analyzing the Job
B. The Job Description
C. Making the Evaluation
D. Pricing the Job

IV. JOB EVALUATION FACTORS

A. Hourly-Paid Factors
B. Supervisory Job Factors

V. THE JOB RANKING METHOD

A. Advantages
B. Disadvantages
C. An Example

VI. THE PREDETERMINED GRADING METHOD

A. Advantages
B. Disadvantages
C. An Example

VII. THE FACTOR COMPARISON METHOD

A. Advantages
B. Disadvantages
C. An Example

VIII. THE POINT METHOD

A. Advantages
B. Disadvantages
C. An Example

IX. PRICING THE JOB

A. Scatter Diagram
B. The Line of Average Relationship Formula Method
C. Eyeball Method

X. DETERMINATION OF JOB GRADE

A. Spread
B. Overlap
C. Red Circle Rates
D. Over and Under Chart
E. Progression

XI. WRITING UP JOBS

A. Style of Writing
B. Job Titles and Code Numbers

S·B·I
SMALL BUSINESS INSTITUTE

Melinda Chevez, Administrative Assistant

January 30, ----

Please key the attached flyer in three columns. You may change the bullets, fonts, margins, borders, lines, etc., to format the flyer attractively. Justify the text. Fit on one page.

Save the file as "getstart."

2714 Spring Forest Road
Raleigh, NC 27610-1997
(919) 555-0126

Hint: Use newspaper columns.

GETTING STARTED
Checklist for Starting a Business

centre

balance newspaper no wid border attractive bullets

- Prepare a written business plan: include a startup plan, a one-year and two-year plan in narrative form.
- Prepare written goals and objectives for your business.
- Obtain resumes for all key persons who will be associated with your business.
- Determine what profit you want from this business, recognizing the time you will give and the investment you will have. Then complete a projected income statement based on your decision.
- Survey the market you plan to serve to ascertain if you can achieve the level of sales to make your desired profit.
- Prepare a statement of assets to be used.
- Prepare an initial projected balance sheet.
- Establish a personnel policy at the outset.
- Establish an adequate system of accounting records.
- Decide whether you wish to operate as a sole proprietorship, a partnership, or a corporation.
- Obtain an employee federal identification number from the nearest Internal Revenue Service office.
- Obtain an application for a Sales and Use Tax Certification of Registration from the Department of Taxation.
- Comply with the Occupational Safety and Health Administration's (OSHA) laws even if you employ only one person.
- Study the location and the specific building or site chosen in relation to specific characteristics.
- Prepare a layout for the entire space to be used for business activity.
- Review all aspects of your merchandising and advertising plan.
- Analyze your estimated expenses in terms of their fixed or variable nature.
- Determine the firm's break-even point.
- Prepare a projected cash flow statement.
- If you are considering sales on account (i.e., accounts receivables), review the advantages and administrative decisions involved. Then establish a credit policy.
- Review the risks that your business will be subjected to and how you plan to cope with them.
- Obtain an application from the Director of Finance or the Commissioner of Revenue where the business is to be located for your local business license.
- For certain businesses, certification by an appropriate board is required. Most certifications require a fee examination and/or educational credits. Contact the Department of Commerce for more information.
- Obtain required permits from local municipalities for any or all of the following:
  - Building Permits
  - Zoning Approval
  - Subdivision Approval
- Check with the local fire department to be sure that your business will be in full compliance with local fire ordinances.

Format Column define

Format Border/Fill Column

S·B·I

SMALL BUSINESS INSTITUTE

Elijah Roberts, Director

February 2, ----

Please key the attached letter. Proofread carefully and use the grammar checker.

Save as "chaseltr."

2714 Spring Forest Road
Raleigh, NC 27610-1997
(919) 555-0126

Reference Manual: Letter Format and Headings for Subsequent Pages

Letter Head.

Header format pg 101 Add line

February 2

Mr. Burton Chase
Raleigh Chamber of Commerce
Post Office Box 1456
Raleigh, NC ~~XXXXX~~ 27609+1996

Dear Burt

During the summer, it came to our attention at SBI that small claims were bing more and more difficult to collect in court by local establishments. At the suggestion of the vice-president of the bar association, we decided to sponsor a two-hour workshop dealing with "How to Best Collect in Small Claims Court." Because of ramifications from consumer groups, we renamed the program "How the Small Businessman Can Use Small Claims Court."

Businessperson

Originally, the vice-president of the bar association and the circuit court associate judge were to be the main speakers. We had a planning meeting between the us, the associate judge and the attorney representing the bar association. The attorney was to speak on how to set up your claims and what advise you can expect to receive form your attorney. The judge was to speak on the stautes in the State of North Carolina and how rulings were made.

In the meantime, reservations began to come in that had never been anticipated. Most of the reservations that came in were from small businesses with less than 25 employees. A majority of those small business people had never attended Chamber meetings or taken advantage of any of the offerings of SBI. On the evening of the session, which was held at a local steak house in which we did not have to charge a fee and participants could go through the line, over 125 small business people attended!

owners ~~persons~~

Unfortunately, on the evening of the program, the associate judge had an emergency that prevented him from attending. However, he

(Job 20 continued on p. 56.)

[was able to send] ~~sent~~ a friend of his who is an attorney in his place. After the meal, both attorneys worked together to give a ninety-minute presentation, which was unrehearsed.

The speakers, who were young and unafraid of speaking out on the judicial system, gave excellent points to the participants on how to collect small claims. One attorney mentioned that in the state of North Carolina, a small business person can even chose his own judge. Individuals discussed across the table, their experiences in Small Claims Court with certain judges, and the attorneys gave their percentages on the likelihood of collection. The program was very effective. Rave comments were made by many [of the] small business ~~people~~ [owners] about the program.

We did not want the local media involved in covering the program because of adverse prulicity that may or may not happen. If you have any specific quesitons, please feel free to call me.

~~Cordially~~ [Sincerely]

Elijah J. Roberts
Director

[RA
Date & file]

S·B·I
SMALL BUSINESS INSTITUTE

Melinda Chevez, Administrative Assistant

February 3, ----

Please key the attached invitation. Set up four invitations per page. Insert a border around each invitation.

Save the file as "breakinv."

2714 Spring Forest Road
Raleigh, NC 27610-1997
(919) 555-0126

(Job 21 continued on p. 58.)

You are cordially invited to a
Small Business Breakfast Forum
on May 8
7:45 a.m. until 9:30 a.m.
In the Raleigh Suites and Convention Center
1123 Fourth Street, Raleigh, NC

RSVP by April 1 (919) 555-0126

Landscape – Format Page

Subdivide Page – Format Page

S·B·I
SMALL BUSINESS INSTITUTE

Melinda Chevez, Administrative Assistant

February 3, ----

Please key the attached proposal as an unbound report. Create a cover page, and generate a table of contents and internal citations from the attached Reference Sheet. Key the references on a separate sheet. Use software styles to format headings. Create a graphic footer to include page numbering. Use February 3 for the date on the cover page.

Please proof carefully and correct all grammatical errors.

Save the file as "proposal."

2714 Spring Forest Road
Raleigh, NC 27610-1997
(919) 555-0126

(Job 22 continued on p. 60.)

Reference Manual: Report Format (Unbound Reports)

LABLE Avery 5160 Address

SMALL BUSINESS INSTITUTE ENHANCEMENT GRANT

(SBI)
The Small Business Institute seek $175,000 in financial support from the united states department of commerce. The requested support will assist **SBI** in developing its entrepreneurial outreach program.

The Institute recognizes the extreme importance of motivating individual initiatives in such a manner as to strengthen the economic and social fiber of the community. of which it is a part. In making the move to the 21st century, we acknowledge that "the localities in the areas that we serve are moving rapidly from an agricultural and industrial economy to an economy based upon information and technology." (1) ~~and that jobs are being created in service and advanced technology industries."~~ The Small Business Institute is uniquely positioned to assist businesses in making this effort.

This ~~The~~ proposal ~~in this document gives~~ provides the framework for an entrepreneurial system that will deliver a program of services that stimulates a lifelong learning process.

The **Small Business Institute** was established to encourage the development of new businesses and to provide guidance and leadership to existing businesses. Its fundamental goals are ~~goal is~~ to offer programs and services that will increase the operational efficiency of small businesses in the Raleigh area. The Institute is actively engaged in providing an annual conference and exposition, breakfast workshops, community college courses, and technical assistance to community clients.

ds Side heading ← Enhancement Program
ds

The Enhancement Program integrates the needs of small business owners ~~these two constituents in a manner that provides synergistic value.~~ and the community ~~of~~ in which they serve by providing research and community support.

Research Support. Entrepreneurial research is a growing field and is making a valuable contribution to mainstream management research. Katz provides a useful overview of leading-edge research and observes that entrepreneurship is rapidly becoming a major source of vital ideas and research opportunities for management scholars of diverse interests (Katz, 1994, p. 13).

Need. The need with respect to research support are twofold: direct and indirect support of **SBI** publications. SBI need funds to provide businesses with one-to-one technical assistance and to acquire additional computer hardware and presentation equipment.

Outcome. We expects to increase the number of **SBI** publications by 50 percent within a five year period.

Community Support. Some years ago, the question often posed with respect to entrepreneurial education was Can entrepreneurship be taught? But as we move through the second decade of specific entrepreneurial education, it is clear that this field is creating a new paradigm in business schools. Entrepreneurship is viewed more as a process than a task, and it is the job of the business schools to support that process. New areas of instruction are being taught to new business owners or those hoping to start a new business such as the processes of raising capital, launching new ventures, and exploring global opportunities.

The **Small Business Institute** recognize the value added through a program of process-oriented learning. Over the last four years, we have endeavored to create an entrepreneurial infrastructure that supports the community and the academic environment. While we conduct a significant number of programs to provide such support, we are severely limited by the lack of a financial budget for such pursuits. Over the last several years, we have primarily financed the programs through funds generated by the

(Job 22 continued on p. 62.)

annual conference and exposition business expo. The revenues generated to support the community activities of the **SBI** have suffered.

Need. The **SBI** needs funds to continue its community outreach program over a five year period to provide direct technical assistance to one hundred entrepreneurs annually, to provide a virtual support laboratory for entrepreneurs to study specific trends and opportunities in their industry, and to provide current resource information to support entrepreneurship.

Implementation. The program discussed here will be implemented in the initial year of funding with a base established for supporting entrepreneurial endeavors. The virtual support laboratory will form the hub for the development of other activities, acting as a clearinghouse for information dissemination to entrepreneurs, students, and speakers. The laboratory will also provide a continuous learning environment for entrepreneurs and students. Faculty members will be encouraged to take a lead roll in developing entrepreneurial educational opportunities. The funding requested here will support seminar program development, student entrepreneurial participation, speaker expenses, and resource enhancement (including hardware, software, and publications). Some funding will be allocated to support travel expenses associated with exposing the program at academic and business conferences.

Evaluation. The program will be evaluated qualitatively through questionnaires distributed to entrepreneurs, students, and faculty. From a quantitative perspective, the program will be evaluated using actual counts of entrepreneurs and students served. The standard of measurement for success of the program overall is its contribution to supporting the mission and vision of **Small**

Business Institute. We ~~expect to~~ will utilize the results of the evaluation ~~mechanisms~~ to make incremental program improvements as required.

~~[1]Katz, John. "Pursuing Entrepreneurial Excellence." Journal of Entrepreneurship. May, 1997, Volume X, pages 34-39~~

References

1) Katz, John. "Pursuing Entrepreneurial Excellence." Journal of Entrepreneurship, Spring, 1996, pages 34-39.

2) Hunt, Bob and Tyler, Edgar. Small Business Management. Cincinnati: Brown Publishing Company, 1998, pages 147-52.

3) Alonso, Warren. "Managing and Marketing Your Business." State of North Carolina Bulletin 4721, Raleigh: North Carolina, 1995, pages 129-43.

4) Eisenhardts, Kathleen. "The Joys of Starting Your Own Business." Money and Banking Magazine, June, 1997, pages 8-12.

S·B·I
SMALL BUSINESS INSTITUTE

Melinda Chevez, Administrative Assistant

To: *Office Specialist* Date: *February 4, ----*

( ) Please investigate and return to me.
( ) Please correct.
(✓) Please take charge of this.
( ) Please prepare for my signature.
( ) Please select ____ records and print.
( ) Please prepare a response.

COMMENTS

Create a data file for the partial list of participants who will be attending the "Making the Small Business Connection" Conference in May. Create enough fields so that the list can be used to prepare mailing labels, incorporated in the salutation or in the body of a letter, or sorted by last name, city, state, or postal code. Enter data for all the registrations we've received to date. (attached) Print the file.

Save the file as "attendee."

Melinda Chevez
Signature

SBI
2714 Spring Forest Road
Raleigh, NC 27610-1997

"MAKING THE SMALL BUSINESS CONNECTION"
CONFERENCE & EXPO

REGISTRATION FORM

Company's Name South Atlantic Body Shop Phone 919-555-0148
Address 212 Fernwood Farms Rd. Durham ZIP 22706-1876
Individual's Name and Title Mr. Gregory Wilson
Registrations 1 @ $99 = $ 99
____ @ $79 = $____ (for 2 or more persons from same company)
Total Enclosed $ 99.00

✓ Check made payable to SBI ____Purchase Order #________

SBI
2714 Spring Forest Road
Raleigh, NC 27610-1997

"MAKING THE SMALL BUSINESS CONNECTION"
CONFERENCE & EXPO

REGISTRATION FORM

Company's Name Gray Funeral Home Phone (919) 555-0113
Address 124 E. Berkley Boulevard, Raleigh, NC ZIP 27605
Individual's Name and Title Mrs. Michelle Gray, Director
Registrations 1 @ $99 = $ 99.00
____ @ $79 = $____ (for 2 or more persons from same company)
Total Enclosed $ 99.00

✓ Check made payable to SBI ____Purchase Order #________

SBI
2714 Spring Forest Road
Raleigh, NC 27610-1997

"MAKING THE SMALL BUSINESS CONNECTION"
CONFERENCE & EXPO

REGISTRATION FORM

Company's Name Williams Upholstery & Glass Co. Phone (919) 555-0137
Address 121 St. Johns Road, Fayetteville, NC ZIP ~~28805~~-6817
Individual's Name and Title Mr. Robert P. Williams, Owner 28976
Registrations 1 @ $99 = $ 99.00
____ @ $79 = $____ (for 2 or more persons from same company)
Total Enclosed $ 99

✓ Check made payable to SBI ____Purchase Order #________

SBI
2714 Spring Forest Road
Raleigh, NC 27610-1997

"MAKING THE SMALL BUSINESS CONNECTION"
CONFERENCE & EXPO

REGISTRATION FORM

Company's Name Blumberg Financial Ser. Phone (919) 555-0128
Address 1020 Red Maple Ln. Raleigh ZIP 27604-1878
Individual's Name and Title Barbara Blumberg, Esq.
Registrations 1 @ $99 = $ 99.00
____ @ $79 = $____ (for 2 or more persons from same company)
Total Enclosed $ 99.00

✓ Check made payable to SBI ____Purchase Order #________

(Job 23 continued on p. 66.)

SBI
2714 Spring Forest Road
Raleigh, NC 27610-1997

"MAKING THE SMALL BUSINESS CONNECTION"
CONFERENCE & EXPO

REGISTRATION FORM

Company's Name Magic Comb Beauty Salon Phone (919) 555-
Address 924 Professional Place, Raleigh ZIP 27607-4242
Individual's Name and Title Ms. Stephanie Masur, Operator
Registrations ✓ @ $99 = $ 99
____ @ $79 = $____ (for 2 or more persons from same company)
Total Enclosed $ 99

✓ Check made payable to SBI ____Purchase Order #________

SBI
2714 Spring Forest Road
Raleigh, NC 27610-1997

"MAKING THE SMALL BUSINESS CONNECTION"
CONFERENCE & EXPO

REGISTRATION FORM

Company's Name Easy Printing Plant Phone (919) 555-0100
Address 373 Northridge Drive, Raleigh ZIP 27608-1973
Individual's Name and Title Alphonso Ramirez, Owner
Registrations ✓ @ $99 = $ 99
____ @ $79 = $____ (for 2 or more persons from same company)
Total Enclosed $ 99

✓ Check made payable to SBI ____Purchase Order #________

SBI
2714 Spring Forest Road
Raleigh, NC 27610-1997

"MAKING THE SMALL BUSINESS CONNECTION"
CONFERENCE & EXPO

REGISTRATION FORM

Company's Name Pellerin Technical Services Phone (919) 555-0130
Address 2432 Lawson Drive, Fayetteville, NC ZIP 28309-1138
Individual's Name and Title Mr. Robert Pellerin, Owner
Registrations 1 @ $99 = $____
____ @ $79 = $____ (for 2 or more persons from same company)
Total Enclosed $ 99

____ Check made payable to SBI ____Purchase Order #________

SBI
2714 Spring Forest Road
Raleigh, NC 27610-1997

"MAKING THE SMALL BUSINESS CONNECTION"
CONFERENCE & EXPO

REGISTRATION FORM

Company's Name Forsham & Forsham Phone (919) 555-0156
Address 4521 E. Honeygrove Rd. Raleigh ZIP 27601-4521
Individual's Name and Title Bill Forsham
Registrations ✓ @ $99 = $ 99
____ @ $79 = $____ (for 2 or more persons from same company)
Total Enclosed $ 99

____ Check made payable to SBI ✓ Purchase Order #________

S·B·I
SMALL BUSINESS INSTITUTE

J. Elliott White, Technical Assistant for Service Businesses

February 5, ----

Please key the attached report in leftbound report format with a cover page. Use February 12 as the date and my name as the author.

Use software styles for the side headings. Number the pages in a footer beginning with page 2; include report title.

Example: (Insurance Report Page 2)

Save the file as "insuranc."

2714 Spring Forest Road
Raleigh, NC 27610-1997
(919) 555-0126

(Job 24 continued on p. 68.)

Reference Manual: Report Format (Leftbound Reports)

Header [TITLE] [PAGE #]

DS

TYPES OF INSURANCE

The purpose of insurance encompasses more than premium payments for policies. The purchase of insurance is a transfer of risk from the business owner to the insurance company through a contractual agreement, the insurance policy.

Your business is exposed to many types of risks. Those risks of unpredictable loss to which your business is subjected are accidental risks. These risks can provide no gains, only loss of your business assets. Before you consider the purchase of insurance to deal with these risks, consider the practice of risk management techniques. Risk management is a decision-making process through which you can effectively reduce the risk of unforeseen loss and the cost of your insurance program. Risk management involves four basic steps: 1) IDENTIFICATION of risks and exposure to loss, 2) AVOIDANCE of risks when possible, 3) MINIMIZATION of those risks that cannot be avoided, and 4) FINANCING AND TRANSFER of those risks that remain.

For most business owners, insurance is the best method for the transfer or financing of risk. The best insurance buys are those that cover losses that have a low probability of occurrence but represent the potential for severe financial loss should they occur; for example, a fire. The worst insurance buys are those that cover losses that have a high probability of occurrence but represent a low potential for severe financial loss should they occur; for example, a plateglass loss. A sound insurance strategy is not to insure those risks for which your business could withstand a loss without creating a financial hardship and insure those risks that you cannot replace. This strategy can include the purchase of insurance with large deductibles in return for premium credits. If you choose to look at a larger deductible, compare the premium savings to be certain that it justifies the increased risk of the high deductible.

It is most important that an insurance program be tailored to the particular needs of your business. It is a puzzle in which all the pieces must fit together properly and leave no open spaces of which you are unaware.

FOOTER (CONTINUED) PAGE 2

Report
FOR
By
Date

PROPERTY INSURANCE

The first step in property insurance is to determine what property to have at risk. You should identify property in four major areas:

1. Property on your premises office furniture and equipment, inventory, improvements to leased premises, etc.

2. Property in transit merchandise on trucks, samples in salespersons' cars, etc.

3. Property on a job site equipment, inventory, tools, etc.

4. Property of others in your care, custody, or control property not belonging to you but for which you are responsible.

Once you have identified what property you wish to insure, you must determine the value for which to insure it. You may choose to value your property and purchase a limit of insurance based on a depreciated value, called actual cash value insurance, or you may choose to value your property and purchase a limit of insurance based on the replacement value, called replacement cost insurance.

When you have determined the value for which to insure your property, you can decide for which risks you wish to be insured. That is to say, what catastrophes do you want to insure against? Fire? Theft? Vandalism? Insurance policies are written in two basic forms: 1) perils insurance and 2) all risk insurance. Perils insurance policies list the hazards against which insurance is provided, e.g., fire, smoke, lightning, or vandalism. If a hazard is not listed, no coverage is provided for that hazard. The cost of a particular company's policy is directly proportional to those risks for which it is providing coverage. An all risk policy provides coverage in a somewhat different manner. An all risk policy provides coverage for all losses of direct physical damage except those specifically excluded. This policy form provides coverage for a much broader range of hazards than the named perils form. The cost of an all risk policy is directly proportional to the perils excluded.

(Job 24 continued on p. 70.)

The coverages and exclusions provided under both of these forms vary from company to company and should be a major concern in determining the cost of your insurance program. Just as you would not buy a house sight unseen, do not purchase an insurance policy without looking at the coverage and exclusions.

LIABILITY INSURANCE

Liability insurance provides coverage for those sums that you become legally obligated to pay because of bodily injury or property damage as described in each particular policy. That is to say, liability insurance pays for judgments brought against you in a court of law when some person or some person's property has been damaged as a result of your business operation. Policy forms must be tailored to each individual business and should be discussed with your agent.

INSURANCE AGENTS AND BROKERS

Your insurance agent can be an invaluable guide in helping you piece together your insurance puzzle. Your agent can help you identify your exposures to loss and decide on the most effective means of dealing with those exposures. Find an agent who is willing and qualified to help you develop a risk management program for your business. If your agent does not provide you with the services you need, find one who will.

When you are selecting an agent/broker, consider the following characteristics of the perfect agent:

- The agent thinks like a businessperson/risk manager first and an insurance salesperson second.
- The agent works for you as your representative, not as an insurance company employee.
- The agent is financially stable and maintains errors and omissions insurance.
- The agent is experienced in your type of business.

- The agent's office is full service and you receive prompt assistance when you request it.

- The agent is professionally trained. Look for CIC, JD, MBA, CPCU, ARM, or other appropriate designations.

- The agent can provide a variety of risk management services including risk analysis, loss control programs, and claims management.

- The agent is a skilled and resourceful marketer of insurance.

- The agent provides an annual review of all insurance policies in force and changes and amends policies as necessary.

Selecting an agent is one of the most important jobs you have in developing your insurance program. A knowledgeable agent can not only help you save premiums now but can also help you avoid surprises in the future.

S·B·I
SMALL BUSINESS INSTITUTE

Janell Rainey, Program Development Manager

February 6, ----

We need to prepare certificates of appreciation for the eight workshop leaders for the "Making the Small Business Connection" Conference and Expo. Please prepare and print one for one of the leaders to let me see it. You may use a certificate template or create from scratch.

The certificate should read (the exact placement of the text may vary, but the certificate must contain all stated information):

Certificate of Appreciation
awarded to
(Speaker's Name)
for participation in
Making the Small Business Connection
Conference and Expo
presented by
Small Business Institute

Elijah J. Roberts, Director — Date

Save the file as "apprcert."

2714 Spring Forest Road
Raleigh, NC 27610-1997
(919) 555-0126

Hint: There are several documents from which you can obtain the names of the speakers.

S·B·I
SMALL BUSINESS INSTITUTE

Melinda Chevez, Administrative Assistant

February 9, ----

Prepare contracts for the teachers on the attached list. Print two copies of each.

2714 Spring Forest Road
Raleigh, NC 27610-1997
(919) 555-0126

(Job 26 continued on p. 74.)

Filename: teachcon

NEW INSTRUCTORS

Mr. Clifton Haynes
234-32-0392
2 Courses
Term: 2d Quarter
Salary: $25 per Credit
No special conditions

MS Excel 7.0
Course Code: CI016-01
8 Lecture Hours and 2 lab hours, total credit hours = 10

MS Access 7.0
Course Code: CI107-01
8 Lecture Hours and 2 lab hours, total credit hours = 10

Miss Patricia Didio
214-09-9383
1 course
Term: 2d Quarter
Salary: $30 per Credit
No Special Conditions

MS Word 7.0
Course Code: CI105-01
8 Lecture Hours and 2 lab hours, total credit hours = 10

NOTE: Use today's date on both contracts.

THINGS TO DO TODAY

February 11, ----

Priority	Task to Be Completed	Completed
A	Prepare my resume.	
	Save the file as:	
	"myresume."	

job 28

S·B·I

SMALL BUSINESS INSTITUTE

Melinda Chevez, Administrative Assistant

February 12, ----

Work with a partner to create the conference program by retrieving the following files into one document. One of you can key the inside of the program while the other keys the outside of the program. You will need to discuss and decide on fonts, graphics, etc.

1. Schedule of Activities - "conregis" (only part of this file will be used)
2. Seminar Topicis - "semtopic"
3. Vendors' List - "vendlst"
4. Speakers' Profile - "profile"

Arrange the information listed in the above order. The names of the speakers for the workshops are listed on the attached sheet. Design a program cover together. Use your judgment to format the program attractively. All information must fit on four 8-1/2" x 11" sheets of paper so that the program will fit on one duplexed sheet of 11" x 17" paper.
Save the file as "program."

2714 Spring Forest Road
Raleigh, NC 27610-1997
(919) 555-0126

Workshop Titles and Leaders

1) How to Get Free Promotion and Publicity
Ms. Donna Sawyer

2) Protecting Your Personnel Investment
Linda Adams, Esq.

3) Customer Satisfaction Program/Handling Customer Complaints
Dr. Vivian Matthews

4) Keeping a Successful Attitude
Mr. Harry Walker

5) Bidding and Quoting on Government Small Purchases
Miss Marshe Armstrong

6) Techniques for Collecting Accounts Receivable
Ms. Phoebe Hernandez

7) Planning and Budgeting--How to Survive in Business
Mr. Wilson Moretz

8) Developing a Marketing Plan for the Small Business
Mrs. Tien S. Sheng

S·B·I

SMALL BUSINESS INSTITUTE

Melinda Chevez, Administrative Assistant

February 12, ----

Please key the attached evaluation forms (one per page). Use your judgment in formatting. All information must be included as written. Include the SBI logo.

Save the file as "evalatio."

2714 Spring Forest Road
Raleigh, NC 27610-1997
(919) 555-0126

Hint: Use the tables function for the first form.

SEMINAR EVALUATION

Seminar Name ______________________________

Seminar Date ______________ Instructor's Name ______________________________

SECTION I

Please rate the instructor on the following criteria:

	Excellent	Good	Average	Poor
1. Knowledge of subject	_____	_____	_____	_____
2. Enthusiasm for subject	_____	_____	_____	_____
3. Stimulated interest in subject area	_____	_____	_____	_____
4. Concern for participant's understanding	_____	_____	_____	_____
5. Effectiveness in oral communication	_____	_____	_____	_____

SECTION II

Please rate the seminar content on the following criteria:

	Excellent	Good	Average	Poor
1. Seminar objectives were made clear	_____	_____	_____	_____
2. Seminar fulfilled stated objectives	_____	_____	_____	_____
3. Presentations were informative	_____	_____	_____	_____
4. Seminar time was utilized effectively	_____	_____	_____	_____
5. Quality of materials was satisfactory	_____	_____	_____	_____

SECTION III

Please elaborate on any answers given above, and give any comments or recommendations for future seminars.

____

____

____

____

(Job 29 continued on p. 80.)

90-DAY FOLLOW-UP EVALUATION

Seminar Name ____

Seminar Number ____

Our records indicate you attended the ~~above listed~~ seminar [listed above]. Please answer the following questions.

1. What techniques or concepts outlined in the seminar have you used?

2. What benefits have you realized from the utilization of those techniques or concepts?

3. What other topics would you [suggest for seminars] ~~be interested in attending workshops on~~?

4. What [seminars (including those suggested in #3)] ~~topics~~ would you be interested in having your employees attend?

S·B·I
SMALL BUSINESS INSTITUTE

Melinda Chevez, Administrative Assistant

February 12, ----

Please add the attached list of names to the "attendee" data file. Add a field for the e-mail address. Print the list alphabetically by last name.

2714 Spring Forest Road
Raleigh, NC 27610-1997
(919) 555-0126

(Job 30 continued on p. 82.)

Filename: attendee

Dr. Meyen Panigraphi
Panigraphi Financial Services
724 Amsterdam Road
Raleigh, NC 27603-1336
panigraphi@fin.or
(919) 555-0183

Mrs. Rosa Brooks
Metropolitan Travel Services
122 E. Berkley Avenue
Raleigh, NC 27603-1390
brooks@travel.com
(919) 555-0140

Miss Arenda Allen
West Tire Company
212 Fernwood Farms Road
Durham, NC 22706-3333
(919) 555-0125

Mr. Tim Farley
Farley Accounting Services
22 W. Fourth Street
Raleigh, NC 27698-1389

Miss Betty Armarne
Symbol-Tech Services
745 Bluecrab Boulevard
Fayetteville, NC 28976-9876
b_armarne@symtech.net
(919) 555-0155

S·B·I

SMALL BUSINESS INSTITUTE

Melinda Chevez, Administrative Assistant

February 13, ----

This is a draft of a study I am writing. Please:

1. make sure that all items are in parallel format.
2. use all capital letters for the main heading.
3. use initial caps for the first level headings and capitalize only the first word for second and subsequent levels.
4. single space the information, double space before and after for only the first and second levels. You may add additional text attributes.
5. change "small business owner" to "women-owned" and "small business" to "women-owned business." Be sure to check changes for correctness.
6. select appropriate symbols for the bullets. Make sure that each level has a different symbol.
7. place the title of the report and page numbers in a header.

2714 Spring Forest Road
Raleigh, NC 27610-1997
(919) 555-0126

(Job 31 continued on p. 84.)

Filename: mentor

Small Business Owner Mentorship Initiative

- **Mission statement**

  The mission of the Small Business Owner Mentorship Initiative is to increase the number of successful small business-owned businesses in the City of Raleigh and in so doing to help develop new community leadership. This will be accomplished through a hands-on mentoring process.

  Specifically, the Initiative seeks to engage the private sector in investing business expertise, skills, contacts, and purchasing power in helping small businesses to fully realize their competitive advantage.

- Assess existing business mentorship program

  The goal of assessing the existing business mentorship program is to identify one or two successful programs that can serve as a model for our own effort.

- Mentees

  The mentee is the owner/operator of a small business who is to be mentored.

  - Expectations of Mentees

    - ★ Must be competitive
    - ★ Must be committed
    - ★ Must have a mind set to share information
    - ★ Must have the need to establish milestones

- Identify prospective mentee

  The following tools will be used to identify prospective "mentees."

  - Potential resources

    - ★ Small business departments of banks
    - ★ Business assistance networks
    - ★ Departments of women-owned and minority-owned business enterprises
    - ★ Attorney and accountant networks

  - Screening process

- ★ A comprehensive, standardized application that incorporates the elements of a miniature business plan
- ★ An interview

■ Needed Qualifications

- ★ Business individuals who have a demonstrated track record of success but have not reached a plateau
- ★ Businesses that can create a competitive advantage and, because of that expertise, can deliver products at a competitive price
- ★ Business individuals who have evidenced interest in their community by virtue of their involvement in civic organizations and the like
- ★ Diversity and Raleigh-based

- Mentors

The mentor, the coach facilitator, is a person who has extensive successful business experience and has knowledge of the available resources.

■ Expectations of Mentors

- ★ Must be committed
- ★ Must facilitate meetings with resource pool
- ★ Must help to access procurement opportunities
- ★ Must review case analysis

- Identify prospective mentor

The following tools will be used to identify prospective "mentors."

■ Potential Resources

- ★ Banks
- ★ Chambers of Commerce
- ★ Business professionals with specific skills in accounting, legal, banking/personal finance, marketing, and information systems
- ★ Attorney and accountant networks
- ★ City officials
- ★ Universities
- ★ Entrepreneurship Centers

- Mentor/Mentee Match and Relationship

(Job 31 continued on p. 86.)

- Mentors will be matched to the mentee based on the type of business, the mentee's needs, and the personal chemistry between the mentor and the mentee.
- There will be an initial three-month trial period, during which time both the mentor and the mentee will work toward establishing the foundation for a close, long-term personal relationship. Should either party elect not to continue the relationship, the mentee will be matched with another mentor.
- A non-compete/non-disclosure agreement will be signed by both the mentor and the mentee at the outset of the mentorship.
- Either party may elect to terminate the relationship at any time, but only after every effort has been made to make the relationship a productive one.

- Mentorship Program Elements

  - Assessment. Assess each mentee's current level of business acumen, and identify each mentee's needs with respect to moving to the next level, i.e., fully realizing their competitive advantage.
  - Development of a Business Plan. The mentor, along with SBI, will assist the mentee in the development of a new business plan that focus on helping the business fully realize its competitive advantage.
  - Address Personal Finances. The financial condition of the business owner or mentee must be scrutinized and addressed. Personal financial statements will be required, and, where necessary, expertise from the potential resources will be drawn upon to put together a personal financial plan.

S·B·I

SMALL BUSINESS INSTITUTE

Melinda Chevez, Administrative Assistant

February 13, ----

We have decided to produce a quarterly newsletter for our staff and members. The members' copies will be mailed to them with their copy of the quarterly report in a 9" x 12" envelope.

1. You will need to include a volume and issue number.
2. Use "Spring" and the current year as the date.

Note: Your instructor will tell you whether to use the newsletter template provided with your software or if you are to create the newsletter from scratch.

Work with one of your co-workers (classmates) to create the newsletter. You may divide the keying responsibility; however, you must work together to select appropriate graphic images, styles for headings, and symbols for paragraph markers, as well as a header or footer for page numbering. (See attached sheet for additional directions.)

Save the file as "newsltr."

2714 Spring Forest Road
Raleigh, NC 27610-1997
(919) 555-0126

(Job 32 continued on p. 88.)

Delete the "Marketing Concept" section and replace it with an article on the upcoming conference. You and your co-workers (classmates) are to compose the article.

SBI Continues to Grow . . .

The Small Business Institute's efforts have resulted in significantly increased delivery of appropriate, affordable, high-quality training to small business owners and managers in the Raleigh area.

During the past two years, **SBI** has organized and delivered training to more than 600 small business owners and more than 2,000 individuals.

A survey of **SBI**'s effectiveness has further confirmed this success. Ninety-five percent reported a high level of satisfaction with the quality of training received.

A review of curricula and marketing materials indicates that **SBI**'s programs are becoming more and more diverse and responsive to local needs with respect to topics, meeting times, and locations.

SBI's success has contributed to the restructuring of its mission and focus.

SBI is now successfully serving two major populations: (1) small business owners and managers who need "survival skills" and (2) individuals who are considering starting or purchasing their own business.

Over the next few months, activity at **SBI** will be heightened. The staff will be initiating an expansion of its membership.

With the aid of technology, the **SBI** staff will focus on the following areas to increase its membership, as well as increase the communication and interaction among **SBI** member businesses and other small businesses.

Cooperative efforts. SBI will initiate efforts to strengthen linkages among the university, college, and junior/community college-based small business development centers.

Curriculum development. SBI will develop training guides to ensure standardized delivery of the following instructional units:

- An overview of small business management
- Developing more sales
- Marketing via the Internet
- Financial management for small business
- Business planning
- Home-based business opportunities
- Inventory controls
- Advertising for small business
- Organizing and operations

(Job 32 continued on p. 90.)

The Marketing Concept

The process for marketing training programs in rural communities presents some challenges and opportunities unlike those found in metropolitan areas. Smaller communities have a number of characteristics that present a unique marketing problem from a training perspective.

Smaller communities sometimes lack ongoing training opportunities; consequently, there may be less interchange of new ideas for business success. Training-oriented communication channels may be lacking. Moreover, small communities face a special need to cooperate, since their main competition often is from surrounding communities rather than from their own locality.

Developing training programs in small communities requires certain strategies. For example, one of the major benefits that small towns can provide to consumers is personalized service. The marketing concept must recognize the social-system nature of the small town. Impersonal brochures will likely fall flat.

In small towns the network marketing process must include the identification of key people—those whom others seem to trust. These people become the foci in developing a steering committee. The steering committee serves as a listening post within the community and as a communicator of community needs to SBI.

Local Needs Survey

A "door-to-door" survey of small independent businesses was conducted recently in the Raleigh metropolitan area.

The 150 small businesses in the survey fell largely into the categories of retail or service and half of them employed mostly part-time help. Forty-five of the owners or managers interviewed indicated an interest in small business training and would be willing to pay for it, while an additional eight respondents expressed an interest in training but would not wish to pay for it. The types of courses that rated the highest levels of interest were planning for profit, budgeting and cash flow, marketing via the Internet, and tax information.

In the process of conducting the survey, the interviewer found that as many small business facilities were up for lease as were operating, indicating that the rate of business failure in the Raleigh area must be at least as high as the national average. Such information is not pleasant, but it can be useful in planning programs—such as "survival skills"—to best meet the needs of your own small business community.

(Job 32 continued on p. 92.)

Resources

Resources for teachers of small business courses are

- *The Small Business Advisor* and the *Small Business Management Digest*. These publications present comprehensive reports on pertinent problems of small business operations.
- *The Consultant's Guide: Establishing and Operating Your Successful Consulting Firm.* This kit defines, instructs, and advises on every aspect of the consulting business.
- *Small Business Management: A Guide for Program Planning.* This guide assists program planners and curriculum developers in selecting entrepreneurship education materials.
- *Intelligent Purchasing of Equipment for the Small Business Owner.*
- *Banking and Small Business.*
- *Contracting with Business.*

Upcoming Events

- Business of Art and Artist Conference. The purpose of this conference is to help visual artists learn the skills necessary to market their art and manage their business affairs.
- Business Over Breakfast. The breakfast seminars will be held the first Tuesday of each month and will feature nuts-and-bolts topics of special interest to the business community.

S·B·I

SMALL BUSINESS INSTITUTE

Reference Manual

Template Diskette Instructions

Eight template files have been provided for your use in completing this simulation. A directory for both Word and WordPerfect is included on the template. Directories (folders) have been created for persons who have documents stored on the diskette. Your instructor will provide you with directions for accessing these files.

The following directories (folders) and files are on the diskette.

CHEVEZ

conregis.xxx*	Registration form for the conference.
ly_vendb.dat	Database of last year's vendors.
mentor.xxx	Draft of a study on Small Business Owner Mentorship Initiative.
profile.xxx	A file of information about the luncheon and banquet speakers.
semtopic.xxx	A file of the descriptions of all workshops.

OHAGEN

crsrev3.xxx	A document showing the revenue from third quarter courses.

TEMPLATE

ltrhead.xxx	A template of the letterhead that is to be used for all letters.
logo.xxx	SBI logo.

**.xxx* represents the software file extension, for example, *.doc* or *.wpd.*

File Stamp

For identification purposes, each document is to have its complete path filename keyed in the lower left-hand corner in a 10-point font. You may use the file stamp command, if your software has that option, or insert the filename manually or in a footer.

Note: In business, the file-stamp information is keyed only on the file copy of the document and not on the original.

Example: C:\roberts\sbiinv.doc or C:\roberts\sbiinv.wpd

Letter Format

Letterhead should be used for all business correspondence. Key all letters in modified block style with blocked paragraphs, mixed punctuation, and left justification, unless otherwise instructed. Use the letter placement table to determine margins and dateline placement.

Date

Begin the date at the center of the page. Spell out the month and use the standard format—month, day, year.

Letter Address

Always use a courtesy title in the address of the person who will receive the letter. Single space the information. Space once between the state and zip code. Use a quadruple space above and a double space below. Always use a zip code, preferably a 9-digit code.

Salutation

Double space above and below. If a specific name is not known, use the job title (e.g. Dear Director) or use *Ladies and Gentlemen* if the letter is addressed to a company.

Body

Key the paragraphs at the left margin. Single space paragraphs, double space above and below.

Complimentary Close

Double space above; quadruple space above writer name and professional title.

Reference Initials

Key your initials at the left margin a double space below the typed name or the job title if used.

Attachment/Enclosure

Key the Attachment/Enclosure notation at the left margin a double space below the reference initials. If the document will be attached, use the word "Attachment." If the document is not attached, use the word "Enclosure."

Copy Notation

Double space above. Indicates that a copy of the letter is being sent to the person named.

Letters

Letter Length	Side Margins	Dateline*
Short (fewer than 100 words)	Default	3″ or center page
Average (100-200 words)	Default	2.7″ or center page
Long (more than 200 words)	Default	2.3″

*or DS below letterhead.

SBI

SMALL BUSINESS INSTITUTE

2714 Spring Forest Road • Raleigh, NC 27610-1997 • (919) 555-0126

Begin at horizontal center; DS below letterhead

March 24, ----

QS

Mr. Thomas Marshall
Gateway Enterprises
890 Summit Avenue
Raleigh, NC 27650-1997

1 space **DS**

Dear Mr. Marshall:

DS

Default SM → The Small Business Institute cordially invites you to **"Making the Small Business Connection"** Conference and Expo. This event will feature a business exhibition, a series of informative workshops, and a luncheon with distinguished speakers and local successful entrepreneurs. ← **Default SM**

DS

Last year we had more than 1,500 attendees and 95 companies showcased their products and services. As a result, individuals from large and small businesses came together, networked, and learned about each other.

DS

We sincerely hope that you can attend this event. Your presence will add so much to making this a successful endeavor.

DS

Sincerely,

QS

Elijah J. Roberts, Director

DS

xx **Key your initials here.**

DS

Enclosure

A:\roberts\invltr **Key file stamp designation here.**

Letter Format

Memorandum Format

Memorandums should be prepared using the memo template edited to include the **SBI** logo in Job 4. Double space between the heading and the body of the memorandum. Key your reference initials a double space below the body.

SBI
SMALL BUSINESS INSTITUTE

Memo

Formats may vary widely.

To: Enrique Ohmori, Technical Assistant

From: Elijah J. Roberts, Director

CC:

Date: February 28, ----

Re: CONFERENCE AND EXPO

DS

Please make sure all businesses that are interested in displaying their products at the Expo on May 8, ----, have been mailed a response card. If we need to update our mailing list, please let Melinda know before February 28.

DS

xx Key your initials here.

A:\roberts\expomemo Key file stamp designation here.

Memorandum Format

Headings for Subsequent Pages

Subsequent pages of letters and memorandums are to be printed on plain paper.

Letter Format

Dr. Alan J. Casey
Page 2
January 5, ----
DS
We will expect to have a reply to your inquiry as soon as we are able to investigate the matter more thoroughly. We would appreciate it if you would allow us sufficient time to do this.
DS
Sincerely,
QS

Elijah J. Roberts, Director
DS
xx **Key your initials here.**
DS
Enclosure

A:\roberts\subseqpg **Key file stamp designation here.**

Memorandum Format

Dr. Alan J. Casey
Page 2
January 5, ----
DS
We will expect to have a reply to your inquiry as soon as we are able to investigate the matter more thoroughly. We would appreciate it if you would allow us sufficient time to do this.
DS
xx **Key your initials here.**
DS
Enclosure

A:\roberts\subseqpg **Key file stamp designation here.**

Envelope Format

All correspondence should be mailed in large, business-sized envelopes, No. 10, unless otherwise indicated. If your printer can accommodate envelopes, use the envelope command for your software, including the postal bar code.

If you must create your envelope manually, please use the following guidelines:

- Key the address near the center—about 2″ from the top and 4″ from the left edge of the envelope. The address must contain at least three lines; addresses of more than six lines should be avoided. The last line of an address must contain three items of information ONLY: (1) the city, (2) the state, and (3) the zip code, preferably a 9-digit code. Use the USPS (Postal Service) style. Capitalize all words and omit punctuation.
- Key mailing notations that affect postage (e.g., REGISTERED, CERTIFIED) below the stamp position (line 8); place other special notations (e.g., CONFIDENTIAL, PERSONAL) a double space below the return address.
- Key the return address, if not preprinted, in the upper left corner. Begin the information on line 2 and 3 spaces from the left edge of the envelope.

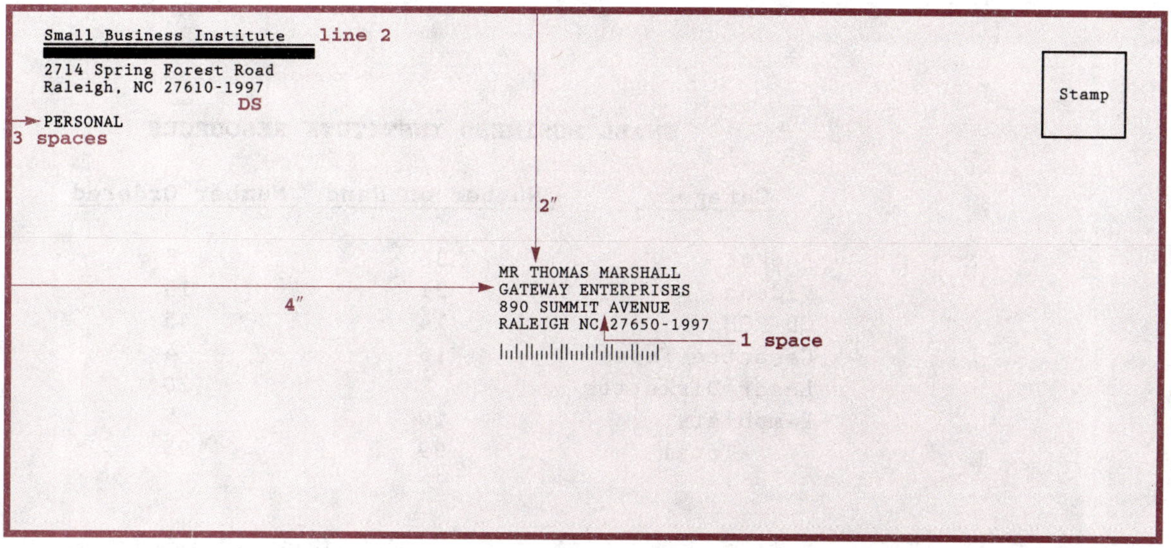

LABEL FORMAT

Use the default margins as specified by the software to generate labels for the letter address. Use the USPS (Postal Service) style. Capitalize all words and omit punctuation.

TABLE FORMAT

Use the table feature of your software program to generate any tabular information. If lines are not required, remove them. You may have to split some cells. Center and capitalize the main heading. Center and capitalize only main words for column headings. Align numbers at the right.

Before removing lines

SMALL BUSINESS INSTITUTE RESOURCES		
Category	**Number on Hand**	**Number Ordered**
Books	36	8
Videos	21	13
CD-ROMs	14	45
Cassette Tapes	16	4
Laser Diskettes	2	20
Pamphlets	10	5
Total	99	95

After removing lines

SMALL BUSINESS INSTITUTE RESOURCES

Category	Number on Hand	Number Ordered
Books	36	8
Videos	21	13
CD-ROMs	14	45
Cassette Tapes	16	4
Laser Diskettes	2	20
Pamphlets	10	5
Total	99	95

Outline Format

Use a 2″ top margin or center vertically. Leave 1″ side margins and at least a 1″ bottom margin. Capitalize and center the main heading; double space after the main heading. Capitalize and double space above and below all level one headings. Capitalize the main words and single space all level two headings. Capitalize only the first word and single space all subsequent levels.

```
2″

                    BUSINESS RESOURCE CENTER
                                          DS
   I.  TECHNICAL ASSISTANCE FOR THE COMMUNITY
1″          2 spaces                     DS
       A.  Break-Even Analysis for Beginning Businesses
       B.  Ratio Analysis for Ongoing Businesses
       C.  Forecasting for Businesses
           1.  Advantages       2 spaces
           2.  Examples
       D.  Financial Statement Preparation
                                         DS
  II.  RESOURCE ASSISTANCE
                          DS
       A.  Maintenance of Resources
           1.  Library of SBA
           2.  Other free publications
       B.  List of Where to Go for Help
                                        DS
 III.  WORKSHOP SERIES
                      DS
       A.  Financing a Business
       B.  Loan Application Procedures
       C.  Budget Preparation
       D.  Automation Considerations




A:\chevez\outline Key file stamp designation here.

1″
```

Outline Format

Report Format

Reports may be typed unbound or leftbound. Please use the following guidelines when keying reports.

Margins

For unbound reports, leave a 2″ top margin for the first page, a 1″ top margin for subsequent pages, 1″ or default side margins, and a 1″ bottom margin. For leftbound reports, leave a 1.5″ top margin for the first page, a 1″ top margin for subsequent pages, a 1.5″ left margin, a 1″ or default right margin, and a 1″ bottom margin.

Spacing

Double space educational reports and indent paragraphs .5″. Single space business reports; key paragraphs at the left margin with a double space above and below.

Headings

Capitalize and center the main heading. Quadruple space below. Underline and capitalize the main words of a side heading. Double space above and below. Bold and capitalize only the first word of paragraph headings. End each paragraph heading with a period. Bold attributes may be added to headings.

Page Numbering

Suppress the page number for page 1 of a report. Place the page number for subsequent pages in the upper right-hand corner. The title of the report and the page number may be placed in a header.

Enumerations

Use the hanging indent format for lists and bulleted items. Single space each enumeration and double space above and below each item if there is more than one line. The number (symbol) and period, if used, are keyed at the paragraph point. The number of spaces between tabs may be decreased.

Documentation

Use internal citations with a separate reference sheet. For internal citations, provide the author's surname, publication date, and page number in parentheses, for example, (White, 1998, 136).

For footnotes and endnotes, use the formats generated by the software.

List all references on a separate page, which should be the last page of the report, quoted or not, in alphabetical order by author surname. Key the title "REFERENCES" in all caps and centered. Quadruple space between the heading and the first reference. Each reference is single spaced, with a double space between references. Use hanging indent to format the references, i.e, begin the first line of each reference at the left margin. Indent subsequent lines .5″ from the left margin. Use the same top and side margins as the first page of the report, but format the page numbers as subsequent pages of the report.

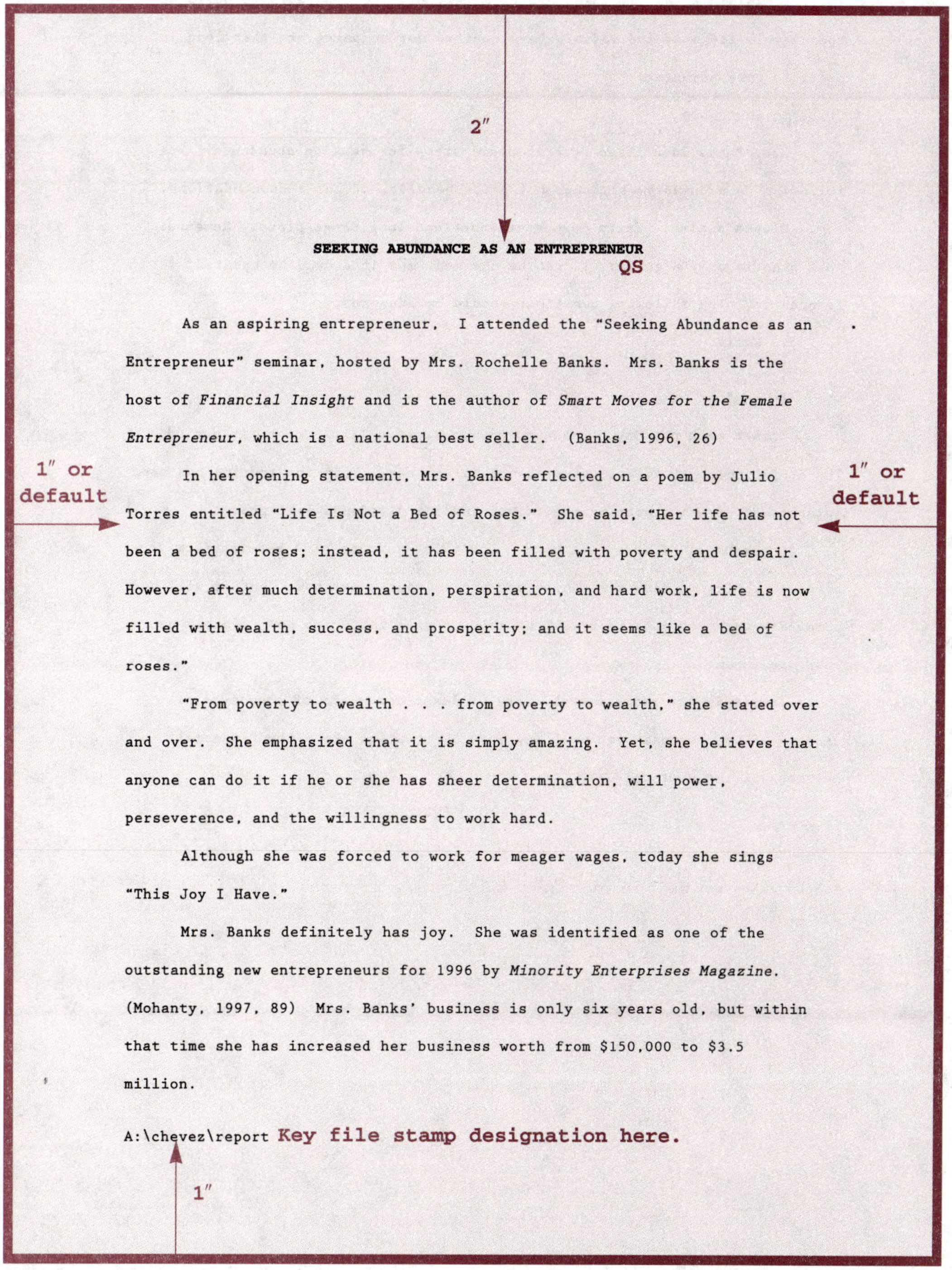

SEEKING ABUNDANCE AS AN ENTREPRENEUR

As an aspiring entrepreneur, I attended the "Seeking Abundance as an Entrepreneur" seminar, hosted by Mrs. Rochelle Banks. Mrs. Banks is the host of *Financial Insight* and is the author of *Smart Moves for the Female Entrepreneur*, which is a national best seller. (Banks, 1996, 26)

In her opening statement, Mrs. Banks reflected on a poem by Julio Torres entitled "Life Is Not a Bed of Roses." She said, "Her life has not been a bed of roses; instead, it has been filled with poverty and despair. However, after much determination, perspiration, and hard work, life is now filled with wealth, success, and prosperity; and it seems like a bed of roses."

"From poverty to wealth . . . from poverty to wealth," she stated over and over. She emphasized that it is simply amazing. Yet, she believes that anyone can do it if he or she has sheer determination, will power, perseverence, and the willingness to work hard.

Although she was forced to work for meager wages, today she sings "This Joy I Have."

Mrs. Banks definitely has joy. She was identified as one of the outstanding new entrepreneurs for 1996 by *Minority Enterprises Magazine*. (Mohanty, 1997, 89) Mrs. Banks' business is only six years old, but within that time she has increased her business worth from $150,000 to $3.5 million.

A:\chevez\report

Unbound Report

1″

Seeking Abundance as an Entrepreneur **Page 2**

DS

1″ or default

1″ or default

Mrs. Banks indicated that abundance can be interpreted to mean a state when you can do what you want to do and not have to worry about how. She further explained that it takes approximately five to ten years to build up to that level, and most individuals have decided not to persevere that long in order to take advantage of abundance.

Steps to Abundance

Mrs. Banks identified several basic steps for seeking abundance. The following is a summary, although not comprehensive, of her recommendations.

Create a plan. Write down your short and long range plans. Remember, this plan is only a guide. It can be changed, and it should be updated frequently. The following questions should be answered:

1. What?
2. Why?
3. When?
4. How?

Invest each pay day. Learn to pay yourself a little each pay period. The amount does not matter; consistency is the key. Once the routine has been established, the increase in the amount and the dividends will grow.

Own a home. Invest in a home. Don't let someone else benefit from your need for shelter. Your first home may not be your dream home, but it will be something that you own. You will be able to sell that home and probably get your dream home.

Invest in the stock market. Buy at least one share of some type of stock. If you buy one, you will buy more eventually. Read the financial sections of the newspaper.

A:\chevez\report **Key file stamp designation here.**

1″

Unbound Report (page 2)

1″

Seeking Abundance as an Entrepreneur Page 3

DS

1″ or default

Maximize your resources. Invest in yourself. You are the most invaluable resource that you have. Stay current. Know what the latest trends and innovations are in your area. Read; attend workshops and seminars.

1″ or default

A:\chevez\report Key file stamp designation here.

1″

Unbound Report (page 3)

1″

Seeking Abundance as an Entrepreneur Page 4

1″ or default

2″

1″ or default

REFERENCES

QS

Banks, Rochelle. *Smart Moves for the Female Entrepreneur.* 2d edition. Madison: Rainey Publishing Company, 1996.

DS

Mohanty, Jarrod. "Outstanding New Entrepreneurs for 1996," *Minority Enterprise Magazine.* July, 1997.

A:\chevez\report Key file stamp designation here.

1″

Unbound Report, References page

Table of Contents

Use the word processing software to generate your table of contents. Leave a 2″ top margin. Capitalize the main heading and place a quadruple space between the heading and listed items. Double space all primary levels, and single space secondary and subsequent levels.

2″

TABLE OF CONTENTS

QS

Executive Summary i

DS

Organizational Chart ii

Introduction 1

Financing a Business 2

Processing an Application 3

Default margin — Preparing a Budget . . . . .4 — Default margin

Automating the Business 5

Advantages 6
Disadvantages 6

Summary 7

Conclusion 8

Number with lowercase Roman numerals → ii

A:\chevez\toc Key file stamp designation here.

1″

Table of Contents Format

Cover Sheet

Capitalize and center the title 2″ from the top. Center the words "Prepared for" 2″ below the title of the report; single space and center the name for whom the report was prepared and title directly below. Center the words "Prepared by" 2″ below the "Prepared for" information; single space and center the preparer's/submitter's name and title directly below. Center the date 2″ below the "Prepared by" information. Graphical elements and watermarks may be used to embellish the cover sheet.

2″

TITLE OF REPORT

2″

Prepared for
Name
Title or Organization

2″

Prepared by
Your Name
Title

2″

(Current date)

A:\chevez\cvsheet **Key file stamp designation here.**

1″

Resume Format

You may create a design or use one of the templates provided in your word processing software to create your resume. Remember your resume is a tool for marketing your qualifications and skills. Use the following headings: Career Objective, Summary of Qualifications and Skills, Education, Experience, Special Skills and Activities (or Hobbies), and References.

P a u l a   J .   K a n e t a

7692 Peridot Drive ❖ ❖ Raleigh, NC 27610-1216 ❖ ❖ (919) 555-0159

Career Objective

An office support specialist with an opportunity to advance to a management position.

Summary of Qualifications and Skills

Key at 50 words per minute
Have in-depth knowledge of COREL WordPerfect and Microsoft Word
Made Honor Roll three consecutive years
Have previous office experience
Have very good interpersonal, speaking, and writing skills

Education

East High School, Raleigh, North Carolina 27510-1617. Served as sophomore class secretary and junior class vice president; served as parliamentarian of Future Business Leaders of America (----).

Experience

Student Assistant. East High School, Raleigh, North Carolina, ---- to present time. Provided general office support. Typed, answered the telephone, and greeted visitors.

Student Tutor. Pembroke Recreational Center, Raleigh, North Carolina, ---- to ----. Assisted elementary school students with homework assignments.

Special Skills and Activities

Fluent in Spanish
Girl Scout Member
City Swim Team

References

Provided upon request.

A:\------\resume `Key file stamp designation here.`

Resume Format

Flyer Format

Use graphical elements and/or watermarks when creating flyers. Vary the print style, size, and font for special effect. Remember that flyers usually include larger fonts and graphics than a general publication.

A Workshop

on

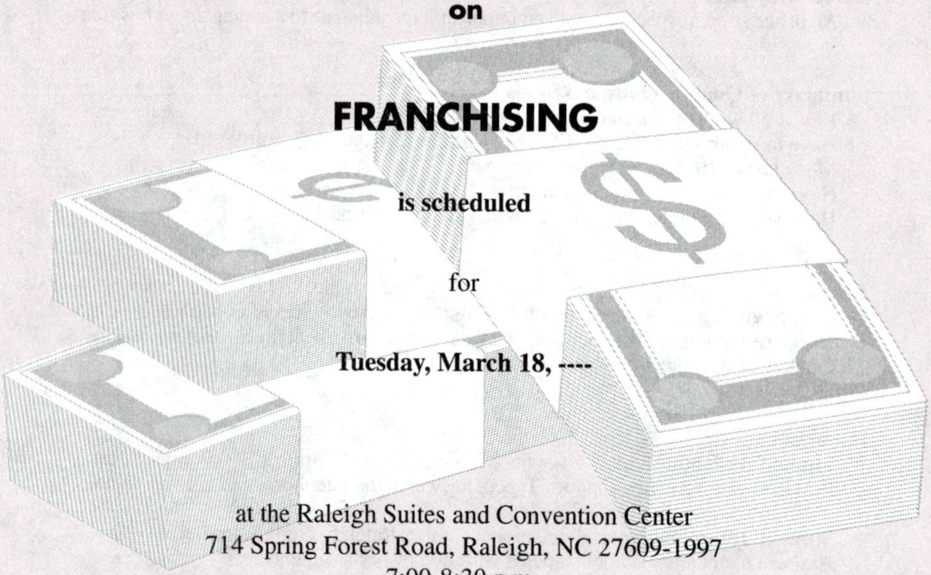

FRANCHISING

is scheduled

for

Tuesday, March 18, ----

at the Raleigh Suites and Convention Center
714 Spring Forest Road, Raleigh, NC 27609-1997
7:00-8:30 p.m.

Presented by The Small Business Institute

A:\roberts\flyer **Key file stamp designation here.**

Flyer Format

Newsletter Format

Use one of the word processing software templates or create a template for a newsletter. Vary the print style, size, and font for special effect. Enhance the newsletter by integrating graphical elements or watermarks.

Proofreaders' Marks

Description	Symbol
Align type	//
Bold	~~
Capitalize	cap or ≡
Close up	⁀
Delete	
Double space	DS
Insert	∧
Insert comma	
Insert apostrophe	∨
Insert quotation marks	∨ ∨
Insert space	# or /#
Leave as is; let it stand	stet or ...
Move down	⊔
Move up	⊓
Move right	⊐
Move left	⊏
No new paragraph	no new ¶
Paragraph	¶
Quadruple space	QS
Set in lowercase	/ or lc
Spell out	○ or sp
Transpose	∿ or tr
Underline or italics	___

Two-Letter State Abbreviations

Alabama	AL	Montana	MT
Alaska	AK	Nebraska	NE
Arizona	AZ	Nevada	NV
Arkansas	AR	New Hampshire	NH
California	CA	New Jersey	NJ
Colorado	CO	New Mexico	NM
Connecticut	CT	New York	NY
Delaware	DE	North Carolina	NC
District of Columbia	DC	North Dakota	ND
Florida	FL	Ohio	OH
Georgia	GA	Oklahoma	OK
Hawaii	HI	Oregon	OR
Idaho	ID	Pennsylvania	PA
Illinois	IL	Rhode Island	RI
Indiana	IN	South Carolina	SC
Iowa	IA	South Dakota	SD
Kansas	KS	Tennessee	TN
Kentucky	KY	Texas	TX
Louisiana	LA	Utah	UT
Maine	ME	Vermont	VT
Maryland	MD	Virginia	VA
Massachusetts	MA	Washington	WA
Michigan	MI	West Virginia	WV
Minnesota	MN	Wisconsin	WI
Mississippi	MS	Wyoming	WY
Missouri	MO		

COMMAND SUMMARY

COMMAND	WORDPERFECT 6.1	WORD 6.0	JOBS
Border	Format/Page/Border/Fill	Format/Borders and Shading	19, 21, 25
Columns	Format/Columns	Format/Columns	5, 8, 15, 19, 32
Drop Cap	Format/Drop Cap	Format/Drop Cap	32
Envelopes	Format/Envelope	Tools/Envelope and Labels	8, 11, 20
File Stamp	Insert/Other/Path and Filename	View/Header and Footer/ **Key** "{filename\p}"	1-32
Find and Replace	Edit/Find and Replace	Edit/Replace	31
Fonts	Format/Font	Format/Font	2, 5, 9, 17, 19, 22, 25, 27, 28
Footnotes	Insert/Footnote	Insert/Footnote	Optional job
Grammar	Tools/Grammatik	Tools/Grammar	20, 22
Graphics	Graphics/Image	Insert/Object	2, 5, 28, 32
Headers and Footers	Insert/Header/Footer	View/Header and Footer	22, 24, 31, 32
Labels	Format/Labels	Tools/Envelopes and Labels	7
Macro	Tools/Macro	Tools/Macro	4
Make It Fit/Shrink To Fit	Format/Make It Fit Expert	File/Print Preview/Shrink to Fit	1, 8, 17, 19
Merge	Tools/Merge	Tools/Mail Merge	6, 7, 23, 30
Numbers and Bullets	Insert/Bullets & Numbers	Format/Bullets and Numbering	19, 31, 32
Outline	Tools/Outline	View/Outline	16, 18
Page Numbering	Format/Page/Numbering	Insert/Page Numbers	22, 24, 28, 32
Paper Orientation	Format/Page/Paper Size	File/Page Setup	5, 8, 25
Sort	Tools/Sort	Table/Sort Text	23
Spelling	Tools/Spell Check	Tools/Spelling	1-32
Styles	Format/Styles	Format/Style	24, 28, 31, 32
Table of Contents	Tools/Table of Contents	Insert/Index and Tables	22
Tables Sort Formula Lines/Shading	Table/Create Tools/Sort Table/Formula Bar Table/Lines/Fill	Table/Insert Table Table/Sort Text Table/Formula Format/Borders and Shading	3, 8, 9, 10, 13, 15
Tabs	Format/Line/Tab Set	Format/Tabs	17
Template	File/Template	File/New	4, 12, 13, 14, 26, 27

Command Summary

COMMAND	WORDPERFECT 7.0	WORD 7.0	JOBS
Border	Format/Border/Fill	Format/Borders and Shading	19, 21, 25
Columns	Format/Columns	Format/Columns	5, 8, 15, 19, 32
Drop Cap	Format/Drop Cap	Format/Drop Cap	32
Envelopes	Format/Envelope	Tools/Envelope and Labels	8, 11, 20
File Stamp	Insert/Other/Path and Filename	View/Header and Footer/ **Key** "{filename\p}"	1-32
Find and Replace	Edit/Find and Replace	Edit/Replace	31
Fonts	Format/Font	Format/Font	2, 5, 9, 17, 19, 22, 25, 27, 28
Footnotes	Insert/Footnote	Insert/Footnote	Optional job
Grammar	Tools/Grammatik	Tools/Spelling & Grammar	20, 22
Graphics	Insert/Object	Insert/Object	2, 5, 28, 32
Headers and Footers	Insert/Header/Footer	View/Header and Footer	22, 24, 31, 32
Labels	Format/Labels	Tools/Envelopes and Labels	7
Macro	Tools/Macro	Tools/Macro	4
Make It Fit/Shrink To Fit	Format/Make It Fit	File/Print Preview/Shrink to Fit	1, 8, 17, 19
Merge	Tools/Merge	Tools/Mail Merge	6, 7, 23, 30
Numbers and Bullets	Insert/Outline/Bullets & Numbering	Format/Bullets and Numbering	19, 31, 32
Outline	Insert/Outline/Bullets & Numbering	View/Outline	16, 18
Page Numbering	Format/Page/Numbering	Insert/Page Numbers	22, 24, 28, 32
Paper Orientation	Format/Page/Paper Setup	File/Page Setup	5, 8, 25
Sort	Tools/Sort	Table/Sort	23
Spelling	Tools/Spell Check	Tools/Spelling & Grammar	1-32
Styles	Format/Styles	Format/Style	24, 28, 31, 32
Table of Contents	Tools/Reference	Insert/Index and Tables	22
Tables Sort Formula Lines/Shading	Insert/Table Tools/Sort Table (Toolbar)/Formula Bar Table (Toolbar) Borders/Fill	Table/Insert Table Table/Sort Table/Formula Format/Borders and Shading	3, 8, 9, 10, 13, 15
Tabs	Format/Line/Tab Set	Format/Tabs	17
Template	File/New	File/New	4, 12, 13, 14, 26, 27

COMMAND SUMMARY

COMMAND	WORDPERFECT 8.0	WORD 97	JOBS
Border	Format/Page or Paragraph/ Border/Fill	Format/Borders and Shading	19, 21, 25
Columns	Format/Columns	Format/Columns	5, 8, 15, 19, 32
Drop Cap	Format/Paragraph/Drop Cap	Format/Drop Cap	32
Envelopes	Format/Envelope	Tools/Envelope and Labels	8, 11, 20
File Stamp	Insert/Other/Path and Filename	Insert/AutoText/Header/ Footer/Filename and Path	1-32
Find and Replace	Edit/Find and Replace	Edit/Replace	31
Fonts	Format/Font	Format/Font	2, 5, 9, 17, 19, 22, 25, 27, 28
Footnotes	Insert/Footnote	Insert/Footnote	Optional job
Grammar	Tools/Grammatik	Tools/Spelling & Grammar	20, 22
Graphics	Insert/Object	Insert/Object	2, 5, 28, 32
Headers and Footers	Insert/Header/Footer	View/Header and Footer	22, 24, 31, 32
Labels	Format/Labels	Tools/Envelopes and Labels	7
Macro	Tools/Macro	Tools/Macro	4
Make It Fit/Shrink To Fit	Format/Make It Fit	File/Print Preview/Shrink to Fit	1, 8, 17, 19
Merge	Tools/Merge	Tools/Mail Merge	6, 7, 23, 30
Numbers and Bullets	Insert/Outline/Bullets & Numbering	Format/Bullets and Numbering	19, 31, 32
Outline	Insert/Outline/Bullets & Numbering	View/Outline	16, 18
Page Numbering	Format/Page/Numbering	Insert/Page Numbers	22, 24, 28, 32
Paper Orientation	Format/Page/Paper Setup	File/Page Setup	5, 8, 25
Sort	Tools/Sort	Table/Sort	23
Spelling	Tools/Spell Check	Tools/Spelling & Grammar	1-32
Styles	Format/Styles	Format/Style	24, 28, 31, 32
Table of Contents	Tools/Reference	Insert/Index and Tables	22
Tables Sort Formula Lines/Shading	Insert/Table Tools/Sort Table (Toolbar)/Formula Bar Table (Toolbar) Borders/Fill	Table/Insert Table Table/Sort Table/Formula Format/Borders and Shading	3, 8, 9, 10, 13, 15
Tabs	Format/Line/Tab Set	Format/Tabs	17
Template	File/New	File/New	4, 12, 13, 14, 26, 27

Job Log

JOB NO.	DATE COMPLETED	GRADE	JOB NO.	DATE COMPLETED	GRADE
1			24		
2			25		
3			26		
4			27		
5			28		
6			29		
7			30		
8			31		
9			32		
10			Optional 1		
11			Optional 2		
12			Optional 3		
13			Optional 4		
14			Optional 5		
15					
16					
17					
18					
19					
20					
21					
22					
23					